THE UNCONSCIOUS BIAS

OF A TRIAL ATTORNEY

A Reflection on the biases of my time, my place, my ethnicity and my race.

A PERSONAL VOIR DIRE

We know jurors carry biases into the courtroom which trial lawyers try to discern and weed out, but what are mine? And if I can ever learn to see them, can I weed them out? I began this personal dialogue many years ago while working for Walmart as an in-house lawyer managing litigation. Walmart had a lot of good speakers on unconscious bias, which I took to heart in my professional life and my personal life. In my job as a litigation manager, I was required to assess risk, and thus forced to try to see "risk" through the jury's eyes, meaning, what unconscious biases were our attorneys bringing into the courtroom? Where they the right attorneys to be "the face of Walmart" at trial or would some unconscious bias on their part mix with an unconscious bias of the jury and end up with some explosive cocktail leading to the dreaded nuclear verdict?

But these questions only scratched the surface, for looking at other's biases is the heart of the unconscious bias problem because they ignored my own. What I saw as a "bias" in others may be no more than a reflection of my bias.

Thus, the starting point is always looking into oneself, and not at others, for the nature of the problem is the fact that I am blind to it.

Could I ever really step outside myself or was I hopelessly trapped inside the time, place, ethnicity and race of my birth? My hope to voir dire myself and weed it out seemed a lost cause, for the nature of bias meant my soul was hopeless trapped in a time, place and race I could not change, but I tried anyway, looking back into the time and place of my birth to ask, who am I?

I was born in the South in 1964, the year the Civil Rights Act was passed, and raised in Springdale, Arkansas, a small town of sixteen thousand people. It was disparagingly called "Chickendale" at the time, because it was the home to Tyson Chicken, now the largest poultry producer in the world, and the neighbor to future home of Walmart, the largest retailer in the world.

Rumor always had it that there was once a sign at the city limits telling blacks not to let the sun go down on their back. I don't know if that was true, but it is true that's what we kids believed and that there were no black people living in Springdale, not at least until I graduated from high school. There were some living in the adjoining college town of Fayetteville, living in a place called "N…. Holler."

And though Springdale now has a large Hispanic population, and one of its two high schools is over 75% minority, there were only two Hispanic families living in Springdale when I was a kid. One of those families had a son my age, who was then and now my best friend. His name is Robert Sanchez. We would later join the Army together.

Springdale has changed since 1964. As a young lawyer later working with my Dad, I met and had the opportunity to work with Vince Smith, an African American Attorney in Springdale, who would later become a Federal Court Judge for the 8th Circuit, and my oldest daughter would go to her high school homecoming with a young African American man.

I was raised by an attorney/father I liken to Atticus Finch. I went to law school, and prior to going, I asked him which of several electives I should take. He said it didn't matter, for there were only two sides to the law – you either represented the big guy or the little guy, and to remember that no matter which area of law I studied, to remember those two sides opposed each other in the application of that law. He said that after law school, each lawyer had to decide who he wanted to represent, either the big guy or the little guy, and I would to. He said that thirty years ago, he decided to represent the little guy like his dad who was a chicken farmer, but there wasn't much money in it.

It's hard not to see that, for better or for worse, I didn't fall far from my father's tree and that despite my teenage rebellion, I ended up following a path close to his footsteps. He became a lawyer, and so did I. He was married for 55 years and had three sons. I have been married for 28 and have three kids too. He was an Army paratrooper after high school and so was I. For better or for worse, I can see how I am a product of the time and place of my birth, that I am living off of my inheritance.

"Unconscious bias" thus makes sense, but it's not really a new concept, but a new term for an old idea we used to call "sins of the father." Unconscious bias begins with the simple truth that everything I possesses was given me, whether in body or in spirit, from the color of my eyes to a character born of my experiences with others, through others with whom I was raised. Even the nature of my thoughts are not my own, they are simply the accumulation of discarded, incomplete philosophies, religions, rhymes and reasons of countless others, for "there is nothing new under the sun", not even my own thoughts or fears.

A person is bequeathed all their being; a byproduct of a long line of untraceable history, of unknown ancestry, his or her thoughts and actions molded through the years by the experiences and teachings of others with whom they associate, leaving no room in the ebb and flow of a life he or she did not choose, or a birth he or she cannot remember, of a death he or she cannot predict, there is no room for an ego, and little room for judgment, for all that we are bequeathed colors our judgment.

    We are like milk horses of old, pulling wagons laden with heavy milk cannisters, wearing blinders so as not to be distracted from the path of our cultural inheritance, a history which has put a bit in our mouths to guide us, and our judgment burdened with a wagon of history that we pull, to which we add the weight of our own memories and experiences along our way. These are the self-reflections of a milk horse, blinded, pulling a heavy wagon of inheritance, to which I have added the burden of my own experiences, which blind me to the world around me and color my judgment, for better or for worse.

Great Grandmother Carrie Lisle

I knew you before I formed you in your mother's womb.
Jeremiah 1:4

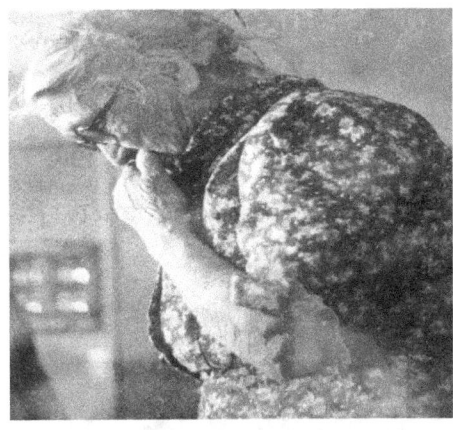

(1979)

This is a photo of my Great Grandmother praying. Born long before the Great Depression, she lost several husbands along the way, but still somehow managed to survive the Great Depression, with kids, with nothing to her name or to help her along the way but her faith in God. Life was tough, but her faith was tougher. That's all she ever had, really, as life didn't offer her much more. My brother took this picture in about 1977, as she stood and prayed in Rocky Comfort Church, an old wooden, one room church without air-conditioning or indoor plumbing.

The Verdict

There is sacredness in tears. They are not the mark of weakness, but of power.
Washington Irving

(Photo of my Dad)

A law professor once asked our class if courtrooms deliver justice. I already knew the answer. I learned it watching my Dad try a case when I was still a boy. I learned it sitting on a hard, wooden bench at the old Fayetteville Courthouse, watching my Dad deliver his closing argument to twelve jurors in a case he called the "Pap" case.

When I was ten years old, my Dad took me to the old Fayetteville courthouse for a trial he was finishing. We entered the courthouse through the basement door. Down in the basement, hanging on the wall, was a big mural, a painting of soldiers, sailors and Marines of past wars. Across the top of the mural was a saying "Our Hope lies in Heroic Men."

Over the many years, many lawyers had entered this courthouse through the same basement doors and passed by this same mural on their way upstairs to the courtroom to do battle. My Dad was one of them. I never forgot that old mural, and often wondered if it affected my Dad like it affected me.

As we passed the mural, I saw the elevator, but we didn't take it, we took the stairs. Taking the stairs didn't surprise me, though, for my Dad had a saying "why sit when you can stand, why walk when you can run." Though his saying didn't mention anything about stairs or elevators, I knew if we weren't supposed to sit or walk, we wouldn't be taking the elevator either.

When we got into the courtroom, my Dad sat me on a hard, wooden bench where visitors were allowed to sit and watch. I sat on the bench behind my Dad. My Dad sat with his clients at a table not far from the jury. My Dad represented a mom and Dad who had lost all three sons. I don't remember the parents' names.

My Dad didn't have to tell me to be quiet, for neither of us had said a word since we entered the old courthouse. From the moment we entered the old courthouse and passed the mural, I could see the gravity of the situation written all over his face. He was deep in thought, and I knew better than to disturb him.

I was alone in the visitor section. I don't know why my brothers and mom weren't there or why I wasn't in school. If I had been sick, I'm sure I would have been at home with my mom, but I wasn't. At the time, it didn't seem unusual to be there alone, in fact, I was excited to be there, but now, I wish I knew why.

Not long before my Dad died of dementia, I asked him why he took me. I asked because even though he had dementia, sometimes people with dementia vividly recall pieces of their past. Unfortunately, when I asked about the Pap case all he could say was "that was terrible."

Pap was a slum lord who refused to replace a faulty floor heater in a little wooden tinder box of a house. The heater was the sole source of heat in the little house. One cold winter night, that faulty heater started a fire. The house burned to the ground before the fire department could get there, and before the three boys could get out.

The fire department found their charred bodies cuddling each other in a corner of the bedroom that they shared. The fire department or police took a picture of them as they found them. Mr. Pap told the fire department that he didn't understand why the dog could get out but the boys couldn't.

In law school, my Dad told me that there were only two types of lawyers, those that help the big guy and those that help the little guy. He said that after law school each lawyer had to choose a side and so would I. He said that thirty years ago, he chose to help the little guy like his Dad, a poor chicken farmer. But he said there wasn't much money in it.

Pap was the big guy in this case. He was the guy that chose to pinch a few pennies and not replace a faulty space heater he had repeatedly been asked to replace. Pap never did, and instead of asking himself why he didn't replace the heater, he faulted instead three little boys for not being able to get out of a burning house when the dog could.

Then my Dad got up to make his closing argument. Watching my Dad, the jury and the judge was like watching Atticus Finch in my favorite movie "To Kill a Mockingbird." "To Kill a Mockingbird" was about a poor country lawyer named Atticus Finch who defended a black man falsely accused of a rape. Like Atticus, my Dad was a poor country lawyer, and like Scout and her brother watching their Dad Atticus try his case, I was watching my Dad try his.

My Dad told the jury that if they thought Pap was at fault, they would then have to try and place a monetary value on the lives of those three little boys, but how could a price ever be put on the lives of those three little boys or any child? It's something my Dad said would be difficult to do and that, despite what the law might suggest, there's no mathematical formula for doing it. He said the law didn't have a mathematical formula for placing a value on the life of a child, but that the law allowed them to deduct from whatever value they came up with the cost of raising that child (that law has since been changed, but at that time, it was the law).

My Dad said the law allowing the deduction of expenses for raising a child simply didn't make sense, and thankfully the jury would also be told to use their common sense. And common sense said no parent dreams of having and raising children for any type of monetary gain. If parents only had kids for economic benefit, they wouldn't have them because it wouldn't make any economic sense. So, if there was no economic benefit to having children, why did people keep having them? Why do married couples dream of having kids and why, then, when a child is lost, or when three boys die in a fire, do their parents cry?

Anyone who would measure the life of the child by how much money they could make off of that child never loved a child of their own and would be incapable of crying at their funeral. With that, my Dad looked at Pap.

"The parents of these three boys cried then and they cry today and would gladly pay any figure you could come up with if, by paying your award, they could have them back. But they will never have them back and no amount of money will ever heal the broken hearts of a mother and father who have lost all their children."

Then, I saw my Dad cry. He was ashamed by his lack of composure and looked down. What he didn't see when he looked down, was that the old farmer sitting on the jury, sitting just in front of him, started crying too.

Eventually, all was said. The lawyers sat down and the jury "retired" to the back room to make their decision.

While they were out, I went to the table where my Dad had been sitting to see the fire department photo. My Dad had blown it up to poster size for the jury to see, but I couldn't see it from where I sat. It was lying against other exhibits, and now that the trial was over, I wanted to see it. While he talked to his clients, I went over to look at it. When he saw me put my hand on it, he put his hand on my own and stopped me. He didn't want me to see that photo. Our eyes met, and though we still hadn't talked since we came through the basement door, our eyes spoke now and I asked him please. He let go my hand and I looked at the photo.

The three boys in the photo were charred black beyond recognition. They were so badly burned that none of them had facial features, no fingers or toes. They looked like boys carved out of charcoal. Their arms clung to one another, showing that in the last moments of their precious little lives, they loved one another dearly. It made me think of my two brothers and me. They were probably about the same ages as us. I believe it reminded my Dad of us too, and I've always wondered if that's why I was in the courtroom that day, to remind him of why he was there.

Not long after, the jury knocked on the door and came back with their verdict. At that time, it was the largest jury award for the death of a child in Arkansas.

So, to answer the professor's question, do courtrooms deliver justice? The answer is no. The Pap verdict didn't change anyone's heart, not Pap's or the parents, and didn't bring those boys back to life. Pap walked out of that courtroom as mean and miserly as he walked in, and that jury award didn't heal the broken hearts of the grieving parents. The boys never came home.

But I did see justice in the courtroom that day, in the heart and tears of my Father who pursued justice against Mr. Pap for the lives of three little boys lost forever, in hope that next time, Mr. Pap might fix a heater if for no reason than to prevent himself from being sued.

As the mural on the courthouse wall says, our hope lies in the heroic men and women who fight for it, and that "terrible" day as my Dad would later call it, and that memory of the mural and my Dad in the courtroom, are forever sketched in my mind.

Sins of the Father

I'm always amazed at how much happiness money can't buy

(Stock Photo of Great Depression)

To understand my Father the attorney, you must understand his Father the farmer, for "the sins of the father" are born into the son they say. My Father was born in 1938. He was born in Western Oklahoma, during the Great Depression, during the Great Dustbowl, a severe drought with dust storms that drove men like my Grandfather out of Oklahoma to seek shelter out West in California. California has a long history of poor settlers seeking work there, and my Grandfather was just one of countless others seeking work.

My Father was born just before my Grandfather broke and ran from the suffocating poverty inflicted by the Oklahoma dust. My Grandfather said the night that my Father was born, the dust settled, and it was unusually clear. He could see a sky of beautiful stars through a hole in the roof above the corncob mattress on the floor where my Father was born. That night, my Grandfather gave my Father the only thing he had to give, his name - Vernon John Lisle. Though my Grandfather went by Vernon and my Father went by John, it wasn't much of a distinction when you knew the two men.

It wasn't long after my Father was born that my Grandfather scooped him up and made the long trek to California. "Go West Young Man" is the old saying. That dream of something better and the pangs of poverty pushed them to venture west. It wasn't an easy trip. This was long before there were interstate highways or cell phones with GPS to guide your way. They chased, I think, the setting sun.

They escaped Oklahoma and never returned, but the two men spent the whole of their lives trying to shake off that suffocating dust. Neither man ever did. It was what made them and everyone like them in their time special. We call them "The Greatest Generation."

Now, back to Vernon and John. Grandfather Vernon prided himself on the fact that he was an educated man, having had more schooling than Lincoln. Grandfather Vernon finished third grade, or so he said, while it was rumored that Lincoln only finished first. True or not, my Grandfather accepted it as true and prided himself on it.

Whether my Grandfather was in fact smarter than Lincoln, we'll never know, but I do know the two shared a common wit born by men who made the West what it is today, made America what it is today, and there is no better example of that common wit than when my Father told my Grandfather that he was going to run away.

They were living in California at the time. My Father was thirteen, just big enough to decide for himself he was ready to leave. When he told my Grandfather he was going to run away. My Grandfather asked "Where to?" My Father said Los Angeles which was thirty minutes away.

My Grandfather asked "How are you going to get there?" My Father said by bus. Keep in mind my Father didn't have money for a bus ticket or a way to the bus station, but my Grandfather said he would take him to the bus station and buy his bus ticket for him.

So my Grandfather drove my Father to the bus station and bought him a ticket to Los Angeles. He hugged my Father, told him that they loved him, and that he was going to miss him. He told my Father that he was always welcome home anytime he was ready to come home. My Grandfather helped him onto the bus, and my Father watched my Grandfather waved goodbye as the bus pulled away.

My Father said he cried all the way to Los Angeles. He got off the bus not knowing where he would go next, until he saw my Grandfather at the terminal waiting for him. He asked my Father if he was ready to come home. He was, and the two drove home together. My Father never ran away again.

Big Sandy

When one doesn't know where to turn, they often turn the wrong way

(On Top of Big Sandy Mountain, 1957, My Dad on the far left and His Brothers)

College, the nearest college, was a long way away from Big Sandy Mountain where my Dad lived his final year of high school in 1957. There is no easy way to get on or off that mountain, then or now. To this day, there's five miles of dirt road to reach the little wooden house where my Dad lived on top of that mountain. In 1957, there wasn't any electricity or running water on the top of that mountain, and each morning, "the boys", my Dad being the oldest, would grab the water jugs and walk to the nearest spring to get the family it's daily water. They didn't bathe as often as we do today.

When my Dad was ready to graduate high school, one of his teachers, Mr. Sutton, asked what he was going to do after graduation. My Dad didn't know. Mr. Sutton asked if he wanted to go visit the local college. It was the first time anyone mentioned college to him. Back then, not many kids went to college. There were no ACT tests given in high school, no college bound school paths for high school students. My Dad's Dad was a farmer with a third-grade education. He never talked to my Dad about college, for no one in the family had ever been. So, going to college was not something my Dad thought about on top of Big Sandy Mountain, until Mr. Sutton brought the subject up.

It was an intriguing idea, and my Dad said yes. Mr. Sutton took his son Bill, who was also graduating high school, and my Dad to the local university at Fayetteville, Arkansas. After touring the school and watching Bill enroll, Mr. Sutton asked my Dad if he would like to enroll. My Dad said he didn't have the money, but Mr. Sutton, I suspect, already knew that, and said he would pay for my Dad's first semester.

Dad enrolled and went that first semester, but he didn't do well and also ran out of money. But that door that Mr. Sutton opened could not be so easily closed, and after a stint in the Army, my Dad returned to college, got his degree, became a lawyer and eventually became a State Senator, all because of the kindness of a high school teacher, Mr. Sutton, who drove him to his first day of school.

But the generosity of this world did not stop with Mr. Sutton. Mr. Sutton was one of but many who helped get my Dad down off that mountain. One of those was a professor. My Dad was a young father, working 40 hours a week at a local chicken plant to pay bills. Having hauled water on Big Sandy, he was used to hard work and wasn't too prideful to work in a chicken plant, but working in the plant didn't always pay enough for him to live and buy his books too.

One of his law professors noticed my Dad without books and asked why. My Dad told him he couldn't afford them at the moment, and the professor bought them for him. My Dad said he didn't know when he would be able to pay him back, and the professor said he didn't expect to be repaid.

My Dad finished law school, but time in the plant didn't leave time to study for the Bar. My Mom told me that it almost broke my

Dad. Three years of working so hard in the plant to get through school, and if he couldn't find time to study and pass the Bar, it would all be for naught. My Dad was at a breaking point.

The next day, there was a knock on the door, and standing at the door were two sisters from Big Sandy, wearing their homemade dresses. It seems they had been saving money to give to someone in need and had been praying to know who to give it to, and the Lord sent them to my parents' door step. With that money, my Dad quit the plant and studied. He passed the Bar exam and got his first job. Neither my Dad nor my Mom can repeat the story without becoming emotional. It was a difficult time for them. It seems like the sisters' prayers were not the only prayers the good Lord answered.

Years later, as a young lawyer working for my Dad, he told me that he spent his entire life trying to pay back all of those people who helped him along the way, not literally of course, but by "paying it forward" as we say today. He paused, looked at me, and said he couldn't possibly live long enough to repay it all.

The Empty Desk

In Second Grade, I sat next to Brian Test. One morning, I went to school but Brian didn't. He never came back. He and his family were killed in a car accident the night before, killed on a long drive home. There used to be a small cross along the roadside where they were all killed, all five of them. The cross is gone, but not the image of Brian's empty desk, patiently waiting for an eight-year boy to come back to school.

Robert Sanchez

A friend loves at all times
Proverbs 17:17

(Robert hugging me at my 10th Birthday Party)

The first person to tell me they loved me, other than my Mom or Dad, was not a girl - it was Robert Sanchez. Everything about when and how it happened would have been perfect if it was a girl and I got my first kiss, but it wasn't a girl and I didn't get a kiss. Sixteen-year-old boys don't typically tell their guy friends they love them, at least not back then, but Robert wasn't a typical guy and didn't come from a typical family. If he loves you, he will tell you, and you will never forget it. Looking back on it, I'm glad that first "I love you" wasn't wasted on a teenage interlude destined to fail, but instead cemented a friendship that lasted forever.

He, me and a few others were camping on Big Sandy Mountain in Huntsville, Arkansas. It was a beautiful view up there, especially at night. We went to my grandfather's old rickety house to fill our canteens with water from an outside spigot. It was a cold night, the air was crisp, and the moon and stars were big and bright. If you stood there on that mountain top and loved someone, you would tell them then and there that you did, and Robert did. He shared what was on his heart. Robert said "I love you guys." It caught me off guard, but I felt it to, and said I love you to. We all said it. Robert taught me something important that night, and that is, if you love someone, tell them. And from that day forward, telling someone I love them became easier for me to say.

Robert and I met long before we stood on that mountain top that night. My first memory of him was him standing behind the dugout at the baseball field. We were both in First Grade, about six years old. Our older brothers played baseball on the same team. My Dad was their coach. I was eating a corndog and Robert was standing behind the dugout talking to "Mr. Lisle", my Dad, while he was trying to coach the game. Back then, Robert loved my Dad more than me, and when the game was over, Robert asked my Dad if he could spend the night. My Dad said he would love to but he couldn't, but he pointed to me and said maybe I could. I did and that started a friendship that led to us standing on that mountain top with Robert saying in the dark, I love you guys.

Robert was tall, real tall. For guys like me under six feet, everyone above six feet seems almost the same size. Robert's nephew is 6'9." Robert isn't that tall, but he is tall. Robert was big enough he could have been a bully, but he wasn't, and that was always remarkable to me as a little guy. Why were some big kids bullies and others weren't? Who knew. It didn't matter. Robert wasn't and that was another something special about him.

He had his share of scuffs though, both then and later as a police officer. I didn't fight much, but in elementary school I told Robert I was going to fight Bruce after school and asked him to help me if anyone jumped in. He said he would. Later, in high school, he thought there was going to be a gang fight and thought they might need help. I didn't know who or what they were fighting about, only that he needed my help, and if he needed my help, things were desperate. So I returned the sixth grade favor and told him yes. We drove around but thankfully never found the guys causing trouble.

After high school, we both joined the Army. We both ended up jumping out of planes with the 82d Airborne Division at Fayetteville, North Carolina. My older brother, a former Army Ranger, told me that there are twenty thousand paratroopers in Fayetteville, North Carolina and every one of them thinks they are the toughest son of a bitch in the world. That was true. Paratroopers have a saying, train hard, play hard. For soldiers, playing hard usually means drinking and fighting off duty. Robert was one of those twenty thousand paratroopers waiting for me in Fayetteville, North Carolina, and he would prove to be one of the toughest.

When I got to Ft. Bragg, my first call was to Robert. He asked where I was and told me to "stand by", he was coming to get me. A few minutes later he came driving a big "cattle truck", literally a truck and trailer used to transport cattle to the slaughter house, but the Army uses them to herd and move lots of troops around post quickly. I couldn't believe he brought a big cattle truck just to pick me up. He loved that truck. He said he had once been the designated driver and taken "the boys" off post in it while they hit the bars.

After the Army, he became a cop and I became a lawyer. One evening, he was going to bring something by my law office. He quickly pulled into my office parking lot. He was a K9 officer and had his dog in the back. When he got there, he told me to jump in he didn't have time. He didn't have time, because he was dispatched to a hot pursuit of a guy driving down the road holding a gun to his ex-girlfriend's head. We found him first and were first in a long line of police cars chasing the guy through Springdale's main thorough fare. We were going fast. I could see the guy and girl in the truck in front of us. When you are going that fast, you don't say anything, you simply grit your teeth and hope it all turns out well. The only one talking was the dog in back, who whined in anticipation of the chase.

The bad guy was busting through stop lights, and we were in close pursuit with the lights and siren blaring. The bad guy was lucky going through those intersections, but we were not - as we went through an intersection, a pickup truck driven by an eighty-year-old man, "T Boned" us hitting my side of the car. The last thing I saw was the front left headlight of that pickup coming through my passenger window. My door folded over my lap and the pickup essentially rested on top of me. All the glass shattered. Robert shut the siren off and asked if I was ok. Other than a small piece of glass in my forehead and my knees throbbing from having been knocked together, I was. The dog was ok too.

When I got home, I told my wife what happened. Since I looked ok so she thought it was a fender bender. It wasn't. It was a miracle we survived and she needed to know it. So I took her to see what was left of the police car still sitting in the tow lot. It looked like it had been to the crusher. Seeing is believing, and when she saw it, she immediately started crying. It was a miracle we both walked away.

Throughout all our years together, Robert continued to love my Dad and I loved his. Robert was not the only one who would tell you he loved you, his Mom and Dad would too. The Sanchez family is a special family that way. Robert's Dad died before mine, and facing death, neither man ever asked God why or cried aloud.

Robert's Dad died of cancer, at home, surrounded by his loving family. I was fortunate enough to be with them in those precious final moments. His Dad was in a coma and had all the morphine they could give him. Then, he unexpectedly opened his eyes, looked at all of us sitting next to him and said "Goodbye." He waved goodbye to everyone in the room as he said it. Then he closed his eyes for the last time, and as he closed his eyes, the candle burning next to him went out. There is no doubt in my mind that God was with the Sanchez family that night, and has walked with them every day of their lives, including the night on the Mountain Top and the day we walked away from that crash. Robert once told me he never asked God for anything, but he did thank him for everything that he had, and I have thanked God for giving me a friend like Robert.

Robert loved my Dad until the day he died. Though my Dad died of Alzheimer's, he never forgot Robert, the boy that asked him to spend the night, and neither will I ever forget Robert, first friend to tell me I love you.

*****

On Christmas Day in 1974, I was ten years old. My dad gave my brothers and me each a copy of "One Hundred and One Famous Poems." He would read us each a poem at night before bed. The first poem I remember him reading to me was "Little Boy Blue" by Eugene Field. Tonight, as he lay in bed, I got to read it to him. He said he remembered it. It has more meaning now, that book, those poems, that poem and that quite time before bed, "Oh the years are many, the years are long ... Since he kissed them and put them there."

The "Hearsay Rule"

Being raised by an attorney, it was hard to win an argument with my Dad, not because he wouldn't listen, but because I could never prove my case. At an early age, and at any age, my Dad would quietly listen to me spout off an emotionally charged opinion and ask "Now son, how are you going to prove that?" It was an introduction into a life-long lesson on the infamous "hearsay rule" and all its nuances that forced me to either quite reading bumper stickers and go find facts or abandon my worthless case.

Billy Lisle

I have always found that mercy bears richer fruits than strict justice.
Abraham Lincoln.

"Billy Lisle was the meanest son of a bitch I ever knew." That's what my older brother's football coach said back in 1979 when his coach learned that we were related to **THE** Billy Lisle from Bentonville, Arkansas. There aren't that many Lisle's in this world that spell their name the right way like we do, and even fewer Lisles living here in "Podunk, Arkansas", so it's a safe bet that the Lisles in Springdale where somehow related to Billy Lisle in Bentonville ten miles away.

Apparently, the Coach and our cousin Billy played football together back in their day of high school. It's funny to me that the Coach would call Billy mean, because that Coach seemed pretty mean himself and was bigger than Billy, a lot bigger than Billy, and since Coach made a living teaching boys to be tough on the football field, him saying Billy was the meanest son of a bitch he ever knew said a lot about Billy, most of it true, probably all of it.

I heard the stories about Billy, some from him but mostly from others, but the stories I heard were not the Billy I knew. I don't know if he was mean or tough, and there is a difference. Whichever it was, if he wasn't born that way, life made him that way, either way it's the only way he survived as long he did. The Billy I knew was a poor country kid, so poor he and his brothers were entitled to free school lunches but instead chose not to eat. They would rather go hungry and did go hungry out of pride. They milked cows before the sun came up and milked them again when they got home from school.

They sometimes broke horses, and Billy prided himself on having broken an unbreakable horse for "The Colonel" that he worked for. No one thought the horse could be broken, not even the Colonel. Billy jumped on its back, bare back, and ran it into the mud where it couldn't jump very well. The horse got tired of bucking before Billy fell off. Billy had broken the unbreakable horse and the Colonel was proud of him.

The Colonel was a retired Army Officer, a hard but fair man. Billy respected him because he respected Billy. The Colonel was the closest man to a father that Billy ever had. Billy's father was a chronic alcoholic, who eventually died in Las Vegas from drinking. Before he died, he abandoned Billy and his brothers and sisters but not before physically abusing an older brother and sexually molesting his sisters. One of his sisters committed suicide later in life.

Billy later told me that being one of the youngest, his father directed his abuse to the others who were older. Billy said his father beat his older brother so bad he would wet the bed uncontrollably. Billy laid there listening to it and vowed at a tender young age of about five that no one would ever touch him or his older brother again.

Billy and his siblings only escaped the horror when their piece of shit parents finally abandoned them in a national park out west. Billy doesn't know where they were or how long they were out there eating out of dumpsters. He just remembers living out there like rats until one day the police picked them up. They were all split up amongst different relatives and he and his older brother were shipped to Arkansas to be raised.

Billy and his brother weren't beat anymore but the living conditions weren't much better. He and his brother slept each night in a well house. The well house is a small building covering the well where the family drew their daily water. Inside there wasn't a cover over the opening of that deep dark well. There wasn't any heat in there either. The winter cold was unbearable and he was always hungry. He was also fearful sleeping next to the well. He was afraid of that dark opening only feet from where they lay. He and his brothers worked the farm, milking cows each morning and each night.

In high school, he started working for "the Colonel" on the Colonel's farm. That's when Billy began playing football and where he met Coach who would later say Billy was the meanest son of a bitch he ever knew. I don't know what Billy did in high school to make everyone think he was mean, but Billy told me one time a big football player was picking on his older brother in the gym after football practice. The bully slapped his brother around a few times in front of everyone laughing. Billy was true to his vow that no one would ever touch his brother or him again. He told the guy he was going to kill him and commenced to beating him to a bloody pulp. He said he beat him with a helmet and anything else he could find and would have killed him except the coaches stopped him.

Billy never made it through high school, but he did get a GED and joined the Marines. He was an exemplary Marine, just like he was an exemplary cowboy on the Colonel's farm. Billy did a tour in Vietnam. His two brothers joined the service too. One was a Marine and one joined the Army. The military was the best life these guys ever had.

Billy's big mistake was getting out of the Marines. He got out, kept drinking like his father and became an alcoholic. He lost control of his life, his wife and kids, and got so drunk he robbed a bank with a sawed-off shotgun. He was a drunk without any money and he and another drunk decided to rob a bank to get beer money. Sounds bad and it was, but something he confessed to me later is he didn't have any rounds for the gun. It was empty. Sounds like a bad comedy, but it wasn't. When he sobered up, he turned himself in. He waived his right to an attorney and pled guilty. Despite having turned himself in and pleading guilty, the judge showed no mercy and gave Billy the maximum sentence of forty years.

Billy did thirteen years of hard time. I visited with him once in prison. I picked him up on a two-day furlough so he could attend his grandma's funeral. He didn't love many people, but he always loved his grandma and told me so.

On the drive home, I asked him what prison was like. He knew I had been in the Army and said it's more difficult to explain life in prison than it is to explain what it's like to be in the Service. I knew what he meant, but then he asked if I had ever seen someone with crazy eyes. I had. He said everyone in prison had crazy eyes, everyone. He said the only life in prison is the memories of the life you had before you got there, and most people had no life before prison, so there wasn't much life in those walls. I told Billy I didn't think I could survive in there and he said, sure you could, you're a Lisle.

Billy was a model prisoner though, so good, that he was put on work release at a local Sheriff's Office. The local Sheriff thought so highly of Billy that he co-signed for Billy to buy a trailer home on a small piece of land. How often does that happen? Billy later sold that and with the little bit of money he made, bought small piece of land next to a river and built himself a small cabin where he could drink alone and not bother anyone.

I never knew Billy the meanest son of a bitch. I knew the Billy who later in life told me to hug my babies every night and tell them I love them. I also knew something more. I once heard Billy, a guy with a GED, tell a lawyer to never put a period at the end of a sentence for no thought is ever complete. I was the lawyer he was talking to, and it was one of the greatest lessons I ever learned.

Letter to Billy Lisle, My Cousin

Dear Bill,

You once told me that the only life in prison was the life you brought with you. I hope you brought just a little of me with you, for you are never far from me. My life outside of prison has you in it. I carry you with me every day, in all that I do, in all that I am. You once and often told me to hug my babies every night, because someday I wouldn't be able to. I hear your voice at night and hug them.

You are always in my thoughts. You are always in my prayers. I don't know exactly who it is I'm praying to, just that spirit world that occasionally sends you and I a vision of what lies beyond our reach, that spirit world that occasionally speaks to us in our dreams. Even though I don't get answers, I feel drawn to it. I whisper to it in the darkness.

My mom once told me that a person never sees themselves the way that others do. She said a person will see from the inside everything that they are not, while others will see from the outside everything that they are. I suspect I see you differently than you see yourself. Despite everything that you're not, you have special meaning to me and always have. From a small child until today, you made me a better person, even though you didn't know it, even though you can't believe it now. Every time you called, every time I saw you in person, you told me you loved me; you meant it, and it made me feel special.

I write this letter to tell you I miss our time together, that I miss our long conversations, the memories of which I cherish now and always will. You can't learn how to make biscuits readying a recipe you once said. You must get your hands dirty. It was an analogy that life's lessons, that true understanding, can't be learned by reading a book. Experience is the greatest teacher they say. And you have had a great but painful teacher called life. You had a hard life and not by choice. I've benefited from your hard life. Though I have the "education" that you don't, you taught me things I never learned in school. You taught me things no professor could, that no preacher could. What I have read, you have learned, and you are the wiser man for it. I think often of the things you told me. I miss those long conversations. I miss your humility. I miss your wisdom. I miss your black coffee. I miss your bowl of beans. I miss your company.

The days are long but the years fly by. It won't be long before we visit again. I look forward to that day. I will see you soon. If there is anything you need from me, please write or call to let me know.

I will not put a period at the end of this letter, for as you once told me, you can never put a period at the end of a sentence, for no thought is ever complete, and neither is this one.

Colonel Barrack

When a boy turns thirteen, put him in a barrel and feed him through a hole. When he turns fifteen, plug the hole.
Mark Twain

Hi Katya,

I'm an informal person, and I hope you will always call me Chris. It may make you uncomfortable to do so, but would make me more comfortable if you did so, and if one of us has to be uncomfortable, I would rather it be you than me, for I am sometimes selfish in that way.

My memories of your Dad are very old, because he was very young when I first met him, but he never seemed young to me, because he was always older than me, the few years difference between a six and nine-year-old is a big difference in those early years. So, although he wasn't officially a Colonel when we met, he was a Colonel to me by virtue of his age, and I followed his orders without question.

My boyhood memory is that he lived in a wooden castle, not a large wooden castle, but an appropriately sized wooden castle for a family of four. It had a large wooden buttress enclosing an equally large backyard, appropriately guarded by an equally large dog named Thor, a Great Dane of old, that commonly slept in the kitchen, under the kitchen table, and when he would arise to walk away the table would rest on the top of his back and move with him, a sight which never ceased to amaze me, and a memory I recount often because of the impression that impressionable dog had on me.

Thor's dog house, when he wasn't in it, made for a great guard house for the handful of boys that would "man" the wooden buttress when your Dad called us to arms, usually to harass some kid passing too close to the house. Your Dad always had an assembly of pre-made dirt clods along the top plank of the wooden buttress to be thrown in a moment's notice. Until then, we would mind the guard house, occasionally chased out by Thor, who thought he was one of us, but no one wanted to be that close to that dog, there simply wasn't enough room in that dog house or courage in our hearts for that.

The Barrack castle, like all castles, had cold floors to the bare feet of morning, but quickly warmed to the personalities that lived within that gave it a unique life, particularly warmed by a mother named Francis that was so loving and kind to me. She once said I was mature for my age. I had no idea what she was talking about - my vocabulary wasn't big enough to know what it meant. But she smiled lovingly and put her hand on my head when she said it, so I knew it was a good thing, not a bad thing. She made me feel good.

That castle your Dad lived in had an array of antiquities from his Grandfather's antique shop just a few blocks away. I particularly liked an old wooden antique phone hanging on a wall just outside the kitchen. I don't know why, but it always fascinated me.

Your Dad's grandfather lived just two houses away, so it's hard to fully appreciate how significant was your Great-Grandfather in your father's life, my life too, but not so much as your Dad's because your Dad was with him constantly. Everyone had a strong reverence for your Great Grandfather, for his acute business acumen and for his strength of character.

All three men, your Great-Grandfather, your Grandfather, and your Father, reminded me then and still do today, of the great men of old, the story of folk lore, the personification of what good men strive to be. The name "Barrack" in my family translates to the great men of old, who lived in castles, guarded by great dogs, who were always ready to man the battlements on a moment's notice, without fear.

Your Dad had a fine collection of soldiers in his room, the finest collection of soldiers I ever saw. I felt like I was in a toy store. I always stood at the end of his bed and marveled at them. They were soldiers from all ages, from Vikings, to the Civil War, to WWII. He had them standing nicely in formation, dress right dress, and I dared not touch them. You may know that, like your Dad, I went to Ranger School. An instructor there told me "you" are either born a Ranger or not, time will reveal who was and who wasn't. Time would soon reveal that your Dad was born a soldier, a Ranger, it was his destiny, his calling, one which he fulfilled with honor.

But at an early age, one does not yet have the discipline acquired by thirty years of military service, and in those early years, I remember Thor leaving a large stinky present in the middle of the floor for us to discover one early morning. Your Dad quickly ordered us kids back to bed; otherwise, we would have to clean it. It was better, he said, to let his mom clean it. So, we waited in bed for her to wake and listened to her gasp as she walked into the kitchen and found Thor's mess.

A lot of time passed over the years when I didn't see your Dad. Some might say we lost touch, but it's hard to lose touch with someone that doesn't change, and time has revealed him to still be the young boy I knew so many years ago, grown now into the fine loving man, father, and soldier that he is today. It's hard to lose touch with a man that never lost touch with himself.

Ten Little Indians

We know what we are, but know not what we may be
William Shakespeare

(Me, believing I was a young Greek Warrior, about 1966)

"Ten Little Indians" was the first play I ever saw, and though I've seen many plays since, including some on Broadway, nothing has yet to compare with the first production I ever saw of "Ten Little Indians" in Springdale, Arkansas.

Going to plays was all a part of my Dad's plan to raise three boys. Now, taking boys to plays doesn't sound like the typical Father's plan to raise three boys, but it was his. First, he had to get us to buy into it his plan. That part was easy; he told us he was raising us to be

Greek Soldiers. He had read all about Athenian Soldiers in college. He told us how brave they were, about how three hundred Spartans fought to the last man at the Battle of Thermopylae. Nothing fired us up more.

We were ready to get started, but then he said something none of us expected – soldiering was more than fighting. He said the Greek Soldiers believed in the complete human being, and that meant a lifetime studying the three human pillars of the arts, the philosophies, and sports. This was all fine and dandy until one day my Dad told my older brother he had to be in the junior high band. My brother got mad and said band was for sissies. My Dad said he knew one boy going into band that wasn't a sissy, and that was my brother. From that day forward, every time he told us to do something we didn't like, he always framed it as part of our training.

I know now my Dad was a bit of a Renaissance man, and he had this idea to expand our horizons, which is easier to do in New York City than in Springdale, Arkansas, a town of about sixteen thousand back in the 70s. Back then, the "Welcome to Springdale" sign was a big picture of a cowboy breaking a horse. Springdale's big yearly event was a Rodeo. It's still a big event, but not as big now as it was then, and as a boy I heard rumors that there used to be a sign outside of Springdale telling African Americans to leave before sundown. I never saw it, but heard the rumors, all to say, it was not going to be easy to raise boys to be "Renaissance Men" in Springdale, Arkansas.

Other than joining the band, there was only one other place to study the arts in Springdale back then, and that was at the "Arts Center of the Ozarks", a small playhouse run by Harry and Kathi Blundell, two college theater majors out of Missouri, who instead of heading north or out west where people appreciated and believed in the arts, brought their belief in the arts to Springdale, Arkansas, where the idea of cowboys still ruled the day.

There is an old saying that if you catch on fire with enthusiasm the world will come to watch you burn. Harry and Kathi were on fire with a passion for theater. The bronco busting Springdale, though, offered little stage talent and had no theater. But their passion spread and they found volunteers, and with their merry little band of volunteers, they started to put on plays in any free space they could find. Like a travelling band of Shakespearean playwrights in the days of old, they travelled the streets of Springdale spreading their belief in Shakespeare. The people of Springdale loved it, and this loving, dedicated couple eventually got the use of an old church for a playhouse, and it was in that little church house that my Dad took us boys to see our first play "Ten Little Indians."

When the lights went off and the curtain opened, my mind and imagination opened too. From that day forward, I was hooked. Like my Dad, Kathi and Harry wanted to reach kids and put on a children's workshop. Steve and I went to that first children's workshop, and after that, we continued to volunteer at the playhouse working the lights, doing whatever they needed to put on plays. Working the lights, we watched in awe as Harry performed as King Arthur. Occasionally, Harry had a kid's part and when he did he would call me. I was once a monkey and later a bus boy.

Steve and I both left Springdale for awhile, but Kathi and Harry continued, and their idea of the bringing the "arts" to Springdale continued to take root and grow. Eventually, the old "Welcome to Springdale" with a cowboy was replaced with something more modern, and that was about the time Harry and Kathi got a new bigger and better Arts Center which became as an important focal point for our city as the Rodeo.

Steve and I eventually became lawyers, returned to Springdale, and even performed in a few more plays. Although we haven't been on stage in years, the memories of Kathi and Harry and their friendship continue to direct me off stage. I'm as inspired now by King Arthur as I was then by the Greeks at Thermopylae.

On James

There is no darker place than the imagination, no sadder place than the heart, no less hope than can be held in the eyes

There once was a small, white, wooden house in Bentonville, Arkansas near the square. I can't tell you what street it was on, but at the time, I could drive there without a GPS, because we didn't have GPS then. That was 30 years ago, a time when there was no internet, when there were no cell phones, when there were no personal computers, back when the population of Bentonville was less than its High School student body today.

I don't know if I could find the house today, though my heart is still drawn to the memory of it. I often think about a time thirty years ago, when a hardworking man lived in that house with his youngest son. The man was divorced. It was a horrible divorce, the pain of which often caused his youngest son headaches, and I know now, much heartache.

He was gentle boy. He was also a small boy. He got beat up in school a lot, in elementary school, maybe high school too, I don't know. But it never hardened his heart. He kept his heart warm with dreams of big things to come, dreams bigger than the little town of

Bentonville, dreams bigger than his little frame, bigger than his bullies, bigger than his troubles, bigger than his little heart. But the warm heart of a gentle boy can only take so much cold daily reality which slowly drowned him and his dreams.

And one cool October night in this little white wooden house somewhere near the Bentonville Square, this single Dad looked into his son's room and saw his son writing. He asked his son how everything was going. His son smiled and said fine. The Dad left him alone to write. A few minutes later, the Dad heard a gunshot outside the backdoor. The Dad's heart broke, and he ran out the back door and held his dying son. And my heart broke too, on that cold October night, in 1982.

His name was James, or "Jaimsey" as his Mom used to call him. He was 17. It was his senior year.

An Empty Wallet

"What right have you to be merry? ... You're poor enough."
From A Christmas Carol by Charles Dickens

Sometimes, it's hard to find the right words. It may even take years to find them, and after so many years of looking, sometimes you never do. I'm not sure I have found them yet, but it's time for me to try to say what I need to say, before I run out of time to find them, assuming I ever do.

A good friend once told me that "If I had a million dollars in my wallet, I wouldn't be worth a damn." My friend never had a million dollars in his wallet, but that's what made him and makes him priceless. My friend had the special privilege of being born poor. His mom and dad were hard working people, but there are a lot of hard-working people that are poor. For the vast majority, poverty has more to do with birthright than how hard you work, but neither he nor his family ever complained. In fact, that's what makes him priceless, he has lived his life with a contagious smile and love of life that money simply cannot buy. So, despite everything he never had, everyone wants what he does have, his love of life, including me. I always have it when I'm with him; if I could just steal it and carry it away with me I would, but I can't, because he holds it in his heart, so I hope he will be my friend forever.

My friend once told me he wanted to be like my Dad when he grew up, to be a good Father like my Dad. I only met my friend's Dad once, when I went to his house in First Grade to play. My friend's Dad died sometime after that, and what I didn't know, until years later, is my friend then unofficially adopted my Dad as his own, in his heart anyway. My Dad did love him as a son, of that I'm sure. Like a son, my friend spoke at my Father's funeral and remembered things I'd forgotten, and with a tear in his eye, said he always wanted to be a father like my own.

My friend, though, unknowingly, fathered me for years. He took me to church, a church called Fishback. It was a small wooden church. He took me in his $600 car that he bought with money earned working at the skating rink. My friend had to work for that car, for nothing was ever given to him, and every dollar in his wallet he earned the hard way. He never had a million dollars in it, but he always had enough, and back then it was enough to buy that car and gas that we needed to get to church, plus make an offering when they passed the plate.

I always wondered what drove him to church. He drove me, but who drove him? He didn't have a dad to shame him into going, and his mom didn't tell him too either, but he did go, and he didn't go quietly, he sang while he was there. He's not the typical guy that sits quietly in a pew while the out of tune but well-meaning volunteers of the ad hoc choir sing "How Great Thou Art." He sang along with them. I didn't. I'm the kind of guy that doesn't sing, but I admired that he did.

He had a great voice, and standing there watching my seventeen-year-old friend sing so beautifully in that wooden church moved me- a memory which moves me to this day, back to Fishback, back to what it means to witness someone love God. All these years later, he has never quit going to church. He has never stopped singing in church, and no one but himself ever made him go. And, he has never stopped inviting me to church. He would drive me today, this very minute, open or closed, if only I would ask, and he would pray with me, or for me. Lord knows I need it, if not, my friend certainly does, and he's probably secretly praying for me, because that's the man he is.

Despite all the ups and downs of life, and he has had as many as any other, I've never seen him cry, not for himself anyway. He did cry a bit at my father's funeral, when he talked about how he loved my Dad and wanted to be a father just like him, but what he doesn't see and didn't see in that moment, is he is just like him. He speaks from the heart and moves people just as well as my Dad the lawyer ever did. Both men were born into poverty, with empty wallets, and both men learned to value those things that money can't buy, and in learning to value life itself, developed a love for life that made both men priceless. Both men became loving fathers. My friend now is a happily married man with four kids of his own and grandkids. I know they wouldn't trade him for a million dollars, and neither would I.

My friend is Mike Fanning, and I wouldn't be a Father without him. He introduced me to my wife and with her we have three beautiful kids of our own. My life simply wouldn't be the same without him.

The Quiet Man

Not many today have ever used an Out House. For those who haven't, and don't know what one is, it is a frontier bathroom. At one time, they were common on farms where there was no running water. The farmer would find a place away from his house, dig a hole, the deeper the better, and then build a small wooden shed around it for a bit of privacy. It was commonly three sided without a door. Inside, there was a small wooden plank with a hole over the hole you just dug, and this uncomfortable wooden plank was where you would sit and do your business.

The Out House was never comfortable and always cold in the winter. In the cold of winter, it was to be avoided at all cost, especially in the middle of the night, but that's not always possible, and wasn't possible for me, a young soldier sleeping in an un-insulated wooden shed with some other soldiers on a cold winter's night in a deep dark snow laden forest of Germany. I couldn't wait for morning, and despite the cold, unzipped my sleeping bag, put on cold boots, a cold coat, mittens, grabbed my rifle and combat gear, and walked out into the dark following a snow-covered path to the Out House.

I was a nineteen-year-old soldier, more nineteen than soldier, but I wore the uniform of a soldier, and it wasn't easy to go to the bathroom in the dark with that uniform on, not with the ammo belt, canteens, heavy coat, rifle and mittens. We weren't supposed to use flashlights either. Learning to soldier meant learning to do everything in the dark by feel, even using the bathroom.

After I finished, I started putting all the stuff back on, but was missing a mitten. I peeked into the hole with my red lens flashlight and there it was, sitting on top of the muck below, but too far for me to reach. This was bad. I needed that mitten. There was three feet of snow on the ground and it was still snowing. The bows of the dark pines bent under the weight of all the snow. We would be out here another two weeks, and my hand would freeze without it.

I had to get that glove, but didn't know how, so I did what any kid does when they screw up, I called my dad. Not my natural father back home, but the one the Army gave me, my adoptive father, my platoon sergeant. For a sergeant with twenty years in service, he was a quiet man. He served three tours in Vietnam. I don't know if he was drafted for the first tour or not, but it didn't matter, because no one got drafted for a second or a third tour, those he volunteered for, and he volunteered to fight in a war that few volunteered to fight and many others protested. I don't know how old he was, but he was so close to retiring he had to be about forty. He was probably about my dad's age, but despite his age, he was up every morning running with us, still parachuting with us, carrying a rucksack with us, and now sleeping in that little un-insulated shed which was the only thing between us and three feet of snow.

I walked back to that shack dreading waking him and telling him I screwed up. I knew he would be mad. He had every right to be mad. The only thing I knew about soldiering was that little mistakes cost lives, even little mistakes like losing mittens. My rifle was cold to the touch, and my hand wouldn't last long out in this cold, certainly not for two weeks. And if I couldn't use my hand, I was useless to everyone and myself. Little mistakes cost lives and I needed my mitten now, and I needed help getting it out of that nasty hole.

Like a good father, he slept little but heard much and as I approached where he laid, he whispered in the dark, "What's wrong Lisle?" I told him I dropped my mitten into the latrine. He didn't curse or yell, didn't even sigh. He unzipped his bag, put on cold boots, his jacket, grabbed his rifle and gear, and together we walked the path to the Out House.

We always carried parachute cord, and when we got there, he took some of that parachute cord and fashioned a hook on the end of it from the fork of a tree branch. Then he dropped it into the hole, hooked my mitten and pulled it out. He handed it to me and softly said "Here you go." That's the last he ever spoke of it – no lesson for me on the way back to our shack or with the guys the next morning which would have embarrassed me.

I once read that you should say nothing unless it adds to the silence. "Here you go" added to the power of an unusually quiet man who had the power and right to yell at a young private but didn't. He never had to yell. He was a quiet man.

The Letter, in Memoriam to a friend, always Faithful

Life is that breaking point between joy and sorry, life and death, pleasure and pain, that moment when you beg for one and run from the other.

(Parachute Drop, Germany, 1985)

This is about a special letter that I received in 1984, and about the special man that took the time to write me, forever inscribing him in my heart. We said our public goodbyes today at his funeral, but I could not bury him today, not his memory anyway, not what he meant to me. That I will take with me to my grave, where our shared memories will be buried once and for all, together.

Letters are rare these days, especially with social media, but letters were rare in 1984 too. Time is precious and not easily expended, and since it takes precious time to write a letter, more time still to buy a stamp, time to find the right address, time to write the right address, that it simply takes so much time there's not enough time to write one and every reason in the world not to begin, and that's what makes that time so special when you're lucky enough to get one. And, if you're luckier still, the letter is hand written and not typed, written in the intimate, imperfect hand of someone who cares enough about you to write and expose the imperfections of their imperfect soul through their imperfect hand.

In 1984, I was eighteen years old, barely a year out of high school. I was far from Springdale, Arkansas, the only place I ever called home, a place that no one with me at the time had heard of, for it wasn't big enough for anyone else to ever have heard of but me. I was a private in the Army, in the Airborne Infantry, a young paratrooper, sitting in the barracks of Northern Italy.

Northern Italy sounds romantic, but it wasn't. It was an austere life. When we weren't digging foxholes, we were living in simple barracks without simple things like air-conditioning, phones, televisions, or play stations. We did have a lot of time to think, usually about home, and I thought of it often while I was away.

Letters were our only connection to home. They were both special and rare. I could count on one hand how many people from home ever wrote me a letter, and count on two hands how many letters I ever received. Getting a letter was like getting a Christmas present. You couldn't wait to open it, and you never read it only once. The ones who took the time to write me are forever inscribed in my heart, and one of those people was David Butt, a former high school English teacher. He was the only teacher that ever wrote me a letter.

Why did he write me? Though he didn't expressly say it, he didn't have to, he wrote to me because he cared about me, cared about a young soldier far from home. Why did he care about a young soldier far from home? Because he knew what it was like. It was in that letter that I learned David was a Marine. I had heard the rumors in high school, but it was through his own voice, in that hand written letter, that he first shared those experiences as a combat Marine in Vietnam with me.

Marines have a motto, Semper Fi, which means "always faithful." David wrote me because he was always faithful. David, more than any, knew the pain of war. He once told a friend that war was like aftershave, a little went a long way. David somehow survived the

Vietnam War. Having survived war, he took war, even the prospect of it, seriously.

When David wrote me in 1984, it was the Cold War. We were always waiting for the balloon to go up. We always had our bags packed and ready on top of our wall lockers. We could be on the planes and jumping anywhere in Europe within a few hours, and the prospect of one of his former students going to war was on David's mind, I guess.

He was worried about me enough to write and let me know he cared. He knew how much a letter meant when you are so far away. He knew how much it meant to know someone back home cared and he cared enough about an eighteen-year-old kid far from home, that he took the precious time to write. David cared about me when no one cared about him. When he returned from War, he came home to a public that spit on Vietnam veterans.

Fortunately, the balloon never went up and I only scrubbed toilets for three years. David was not so fortunate. He fought for his life as a young Marine in a god forsaken jungle hellhole. He fought in a war without humanity but somehow found his and returned with it. He and the others that were fortunate enough to return were not welcomed back.

David's 1984 letter began a special friendship for me. I was always sure to see him when I returned home, and over the years would try to have lunch with as time permitted, but there is never enough time to spend with people who care, and I did not spend enough time with him. I thanked him on Veteran's Day for his service. I hope he knows how special he was.

At David's service today, they said he died having never married, having never had any children. As a lawyer, I respectfully disagree with that. Anyone can father a child, but not everyone can be a father to a child. Though David may not have fathered a child, writing a letter to a kid in 1984 is the kind of thing that a father does, and in that letter and in our friendship thereafter, he fathered me, and not just me, but many other students of his.

David Butt always faithful, always faithful to his country, always faithful to his students, always faithful to his friends. Semper Fi to you David Butt, my loving father, from one of your loving sons, until we meet again, and we shall.

Rex

(Photo of my brother Rex, about 1980)

Rex means King in Latin, and growing up Rex ruled my life like a King. Rex was my big brother, both literally and figuratively. I was the second child, and as the saying goes, second place is the first loser, one of Rex's favorite quotes.

When we were young, my renaissance Father told us he was raising us to be Greek Warriors. He didn't mean this literally of course. He meant it metaphorically, but it didn't work. He couldn't change the way we were born. Rex was born a Spartan. I was born the middle child, much more democratic, born an Athenian.

Rex took his Spartan training seriously and growing up would dish it out by sitting on my chest, holding my mouth open, and letting a ball of spit slowly drip from his mouth into mine. Then, he would close my mouth and blow into my nose like a cat to make me swallow it. After I swallowed, I would yell in anger that when I got bigger than him, I would beat him up. Using his Socratic logic, he would tell me if I was going to do that then, he would have to get all his licks in now while he still could. I learned to keep my mouth shut and waited for the day I got bigger than him. I never did.

I know it will be hard for you to understand, but despite it all, he was an icon to me, something akin to King Leonidas who led the Spartans at the Battle of Thermopylae. I would have followed him and died along side of Rex anywhere. And follow him I did to the Army. He became a Ranger, and eventually I did too. Here's the caveat. I went to Ranger School, but didn't serve in a Ranger unit.

According to Rex, the Rangers, and the rest of the Spartans like him, there's a big difference between going to Ranger School and being in a Ranger unit. Going to Ranger School is not the same as being in a Ranger unit. If an Athenian goes to Sparta to train, it doesn't turn the Athenian into a Spartan. That's how Rex saw it, and despite the fact that I served my country and went to Ranger School, I was and would always be an Athenian, and he would always be Rex, my King.

So, despite all that I had done, I would never be his equal. Life, would though, force him to tolerate his little brother following him around like a lap dog.

After active service, I followed him to a Special Forces Reserve unit. It was almost too much for him. He didn't want to be that close to me and wanted me to keep my distance, but not even Rex can have his way with the Army, and the Army made us sit next to each other on our first night parachute drop serving in the same unit. It came as a surprise to him when they read the loading manifest, and lo and behold, he was going to have to sit next to me on the plane, which meant exit the plane next to me, literally jumping out of the plane within a second of each other.

When we sat next to each other on the plane, he was pissed. He said "You're going to get me killed you non jumping M***** F*****." Why the disdain? I thought to myself. Why the continued lack of respect? I had been jumping for over three years and never killed anyone on a jump, never even gotten close to being tangled with another jumper, but Rex was sure I was going to kill him tonight. "You better stay away from me" was the last thing he said to me before the engines were so loud I couldn't hear him anymore, nor did I want to.

Unfortunately, he planted a seed of doubt in my mind. I had never been worried about a mid air entanglement, but I was tonight. How could he get in my head so easily? The jump master stood us up. We hooked our static lines to the long cable above our heads. I was behind Rex and had to check his equipment. He visibly shook his head negatively like he didn't believe I knew how to check him right. Eventually, the doors were open, the light turned green, and we were running for the back door. I saw him exit, and then I jumped too, closely behind.

I counted to five and checked my chute. I could see it above me, fully deployed. For those five seconds, I forgot about running into Rex, until I heard a voice screaming out through the night sky "Slip away you M**** F****). It was Rex. Rex was screaming at me to slip away, meaning turn my chute and avoid him.

There in front of me, was the shadow of another jumper – Rex. But it wasn't my fault, it was his, but King Rex thought he ruled the sky I guess. He slipped away from no one.

I dared not yell anything back for fear he would recognize my voice. So I slipped away and silently went around him. I hoped to avoid not only a mid air collision, but avoid him thinking I was a non-jumping you know what. As I silently passed by him, he screamed "Is that you Chris?" I said nothing. Then he shouted "That's you isn't it!" I passed away and tried to get as far away from him as I could. I wasn't going to admit anything and wanted to land and have plausible deniability, act like I didn't know what he was talking about.

When I hit the ground, I forgot about Rex. I forgot about Rex because I literally landed next to a big sheered tree, about six feet long, shaped like a spear. I lay there still in my chute and equipment, and looked at the giant spear reaching up to the sky waiting to impale some poor jumper on it. I was lucky. I almost died a painfully horrible death.

Then Rex was there, towering above me. He was getting ready to yell at me when he noticed the giant spear beside me. For the first time in my life, the tone of his voice changed and he kind of said something nice. "You almost got killed." Then, instead of sitting on my chest and spitting in my mouth, he held out his hand and helped me off the ground. "Let's grab your shit and go."

We grabbed my shit and left. I followed him off the drop zone and would follow him anywhere.

Bevo the Bull

Since you cannot see your own face without a mirror, be sure to surround yourself with the reflection of those you love

(Photo of my brother Steve on right and me on the left. Photo taken during Infantry Officer Course, 1990)

Bevo is a magnificent animal. He is the mascot of the Texas Longhorns. Bevo fearlessly charges into hostile stadiums rallying his troops to battle. Whether you like the Longhorns or not, it's hard not to admire Bevo. Little did I know that one day, I would be in a hostile stadium standing next to Bevo. And boy would I thank God for him.

Depending on who you are talking to, Bevo is either the mascot of the Texas Longhorns or my "little" brother Steve. If you say Bevo to anyone in my family, we'll know you're talking about Steve.

It's a nickname that stuck with Steve ever since he first laid eyes on the real Bevo at Razorback Stadium.

We were kids sitting in the grass in the north end zone. We were eating peanuts out of a white paper bag waiting for the teams to take the field. All of the sudden, in all his majestic glory, Bevo came storming out, huffing, puffing and throwing his head as he took the field. Steve was in awe of that big Longhorn. He loved Bevo more than he loved the game. He couldn't quit pointing at him and talking about him. It must have been his spirit animal. Our little "Stevo" quickly turned to "Bevo." My mom said the nickname fitted him, as Steve was bullheaded, but how many five-year olds are not?

Even though I was two years older than Steve, early on we were about the same size and everyone thought we were twins. It didn't take long before he was bigger than me, even in elementary school. We shared a room for the first eighteen years of our lives which made it easy to wear his hand me downs as he outgrew me.

We bonded like brothers always do sharing a room, fighting each other and coming together to fight our mutual enemy, our bigger brother Rex. When we weren't fighting, we were setting door traps above our bedroom door to catch our helpless Mom. One night, we went too far. We balanced a metal trash can above the door so that it would fall on her when she opened the door. We called her to our room and it worked perfectly. But when her knees buckled and she hit the floor, I thought we killed her. We never did that again.

Then, one day, our eighteen years fighting together and against each other were over. I graduated high school and went to the Army. After Steve graduated high school, he joined the National Guard as a Cavalry Scout.

Brothers are never long separated, and as fate would have it, in 1990 we would room together once more for nine weeks at Ft. Benning, Georgia, or "Ft. Beginning" as trainees call it. Ft. Benning is affectionately known as the "school for bad boys, " for those like me too dumb to want a career in the real world. Ft. Benning is the training center for all US Army Infantry soldiers, where the US Government takes young men full of testosterone and channels all that aggression towards some unknown future enemy.

Though I had already been to Ft. Benning several times in my life, this time I was going to the Infantry Officer Course, and this time I was going with my brother Steve.

We were housed in old officer barracks that surrounded a parade field. It wasn't quite like Razorback Stadium today, but probably looked something like it 100 years ago. Like all good training grounds, it was a private place, out of sight of the public eye, where young men were encouraged to pursue the art of war by learning on each other.

Even in our "downtime," we soldiers played various "Reindeer" games for fun. These games always ended with someone being thrown flat on their back. Our Reindeer games weren't anything taught by the US Army and weren't anything sophisticated, but were simple tactics learned on the elementary school playground. You know, find someone on the playground talking to a friend, sneak up behind them, get down on all fours, and let the person they are talking to push them over landing flat on their back. It always makes for a good laugh. But people catch on quickly, and it gets harder to pull off simple tricks, so the game must change. For us, we simply started tackling and dog piling the unwary in our platoon.

One day, a guy from another platoon was in our area, at least I thought he was. There are no lines drawn in the grass to denote boundaries, but he was pushing the unofficial boundaries and deserved to be tackled, so I tackled him. I tackled him and screamed dog pile, and everyone piled on.

It was a good show of force to protect our borders and ward off future intruders. We all laughed. His feelings got hurt, but there was nothing he could do about it. There were too many of us. So he ran off and told his platoon. This little incident led to a war of sorts between our two platoons, escalating over the weeks and growing vastly out of proportion to the little dog pile incident that started it.

The long simmering war finally boiled over on graduation day. There were a few incidents between us on our final morning run, but it all came to a head after the run. After our run, Steve and I were ambushed by this other platoon.

They quickly surrounded us as we walked off the parade field. I don't know if it was their entire platoon, but it sure seemed like it. There were too many to count and in the heat of the moment, I was more worried about being punched than counting. There were guys on all sides of us jeering, working themselves up into a nice lather of hostility, into a berserker frenzy, licking their chops at the prospect of getting a little payback by whipping these Arkansas boys' asses.

I was pissed. I wasn't pissed that they wanted to kick our asses. I was pissed that I couldn't see any of our boys there to help and even out the odds a bit. This couldn't end well for Steve and me. For the first time, I understood what General Custer and his brother Tom might have felt at the Little Bighorn. I didn't think we would die, but I sure thought I was going to get the hell kicked out of me.

In my moment of despair, I heard the Cavalry. Not just any Cavalry, I heard Bevo the Bull coming to life in that hostile stadium. My Dad once said hit the biggest guy first. Steve surely listened. All their troopers were rallying behind some big "muscle head" who's famous last words were "I'm going to send you Lisle boys to the hospital. Which one of you wants to go first?" From the looks of it, he could back it up.

That's when Bevo finally snorted. Bevo said "I'm tired of your shit." Bevo pushed Muscle Head back a couple of steps. Muscle Head got down into some kind of fighting stance and charged head first into Bevo. Bevo gored that Muscle Head with a quick elbow strike to the face that split big dude's face from the corner of his lip to his nostrils. It wasn't pretty.

Muscle Head then went for a leg take down and Bevo flipped him over, judo style, and put him in a rear naked choke. There was no letting this guy tap out. He was turning purple when a big black Captain, one of our instructors, broke through the crowd and pulled Bevo off. Thanks to Bevo, Muscle Head went to the hospital, not the Lisle boys. And the best thing about it all? I never got touched.

The show over, the crowd quickly cleared, and Steve and I stood alone as our Captain now walked up. It didn't look promising. Our hearts sank. We knew we were in trouble. He said the Colonel saw the whole thing. When he said that, my heart sank further still. I just knew we wouldn't be allowed to graduate, but even so, it was worth it standing there in the stadium next to Bevo. Then, the Captain said, "But don't worry. The Colonel said that's what happens when you hone your men into a fine cutting edge."

I'm glad the Colonel took credit for all that fighting spirit, but that's not what happened. He didn't home Steve. That was Bevo. And what I learned over the last eighteen years plus of my life, is that if you mess with Bevo the Bull, you're going to get the horns. The Colonel had nothing to do with it.

This above picture is of Steve aka "Bevo" and me in the summer of 1990 taken in the field at the Infantry Officer's Course. I think it's the only picture of us during that time. I'm on the left and he's on the right.

New Lieutenant

I was a new Lieutenant, but not a new soldier, and any veteran could read the patches on my uniform and know that I had several years as an enlisted soldier under my belt before becoming an officer. I wore the Ranger School Patch, Army Parachute Wings, Expert Infantryman's Badge, and others from my three years of active duty as a paratrooper and three years in a Special Forces Reserve unit.

My first duty assignment as a rifle platoon leader was with the Arkansas National Guard. I was assigned a platoon down in Dequeen, Arkansas, which is in the deep south of Arkansas, and "country" even by the standards of that small state. When I arrived, my platoon was in the field, the woods, and I had the old platoon sergeant gather them together for me to introduce myself. In the woods, in camouflage uniforms with gear, it's impossible to read everyone's name tags, rank, so I had them each tell me their name and how long they had been in service. One of the last men to introduce himself was an "older" black soldier. I don't remember his name, but he said my name is "Specialist _____ and I've been in service for 18 years." Did I hear that right? He had been in service for eighteen years and never made it to sergeant? How as that even possible.

"You've been in service for 18 years?" I asked.

"Yes, Sir" he replied.

"So, you were in Vietnam?"

"Yes Sir. In the Navy."

"Have you been to the NCO school?" This is the mandatory school to be promoted to sergeant.

"Yes, Sir."

I knew there was a problem. Under current Army regulations, if a soldier successfully completed the NCO course it was an automatic promotion to sergeant if there was an open position, and I could see within my ranks there was an open position. I told him I would talk to him later.

After the platoon was dismissed, I asked my platoon sergeant if all that was true. He said it was. When I asked why he hadn't been promoted, he said "He's not leadership material." I explained the Army made that decision when they made it a mandatory promotion taking that decision out of our hands. I said I would bring it up with the Company Commander, the Captain I had yet to meet, and dreading the fact that his introduction to his new lieutenant would throw him into a conflict with one of his sergeants, when so much deference is given them by the Officer Corps.

My platoon sergeant proceeded to educate me about officers, and explained to me how there are two types of officers, the ones that learn to trust their NCOs and the others, meaning me. He referred to a Lieutenant in another platoon that knew how to get along, and fortunately for me, in that moment, that grossly overweight Lieutenant was bending over about 50 yards away with his love handles and butt crack exposed for all to see. I told the Sergeant if that was the kind of officer that he wanted me to be, that would never be me.

The next morning, we were served a hot breakfast in the field. The guys serving were allowed to serve wearing t-shirts. I was going through the line when one of the soldiers putting eggs on my tray said "Sir, you need to slow down." When I asked what he meant, he said "I just mean you need to slow down."

I had no idea who he was, as I had never met him, and didn't know his name because he was wearing an army issue brown t-shirt, not the blouse with the name tag. I did know he wasn't in my platoon.

"Are you threatening me?" I asked.

"I'm just telling you to slow down."

"I take that as a threat, and will remember that you threatened me." I said and walked away.

After breakfast, the Company Commander called for me. He and the 1st Sergeant and my platoon sergeant were waiting for me next to his Humvee. He wanted to know about the promotion issue. I explained. Then the First Sergeant regurgitated what my Platoon Sergeant said yesterday, that they didn't think he was NCO material.

The Company Commander was in a decision vice. He looked to me for any reply I may have. Being a young lawyer in private practice helped, I think, as these guys knew I was an attorney, and used to arguing the law in court, even if that courtroom was now on the side of a dusty road in Dequeen, Arkansas in front of a Company Commander, my judge. When the law is on your side, argue the law, so I fell back on the law of the case, Army Regulation, and repeated that promotion decisions were Officer decisions, and that the regulation was mandatory. He said he would look into it, or as judges say, take it under advisement.

The next month, at my next weekend drill, it was announced that eighteen-year specialist would be promoted to sergeant. It was also announced that my platoon sergeant retired. The Platoon Sergeant apparently didn't want me as a Lieutenant, but he retired too soon, I think, as I was transferred out of the platoon, transferred from an infantry platoon leader to a chemical officer position. Though not a demotion, it was a legal quid pro quo, I think. It was a transfer to a position with no future opportunity and a sign of their disapproval of this new Lieutenant. In the platoon I was leaving, there were three black soldiers out of about 25. When I left, after eighteen years, the one would be promoted to sergeant, and the old platoon sergeant who was retired was replaced with the next highest-ranking sergeant, a black sergeant.

    After the news of my reassignment, I took the walk of shame from the guard house to my car. The "old" specialist met me in the parking lot and handed me a pin from his time in the Navy. I've since lost that pin, but not the memory.

The Chief

Among other things, a former Springdale Chief of Police used to carry a KKK coin and watch porn on his computer at work. An anonymous police officer filed a complaint against the Chief with the Mayor. A local news reporter with ears in the department learned of the complaint and ran the story. Instead of investigating the allegations, the Mayor at the time instructed the Chief to open an internal investigation to ascertain the identity of this anonymous complainant. That anonymous complainant then came to me, scared of losing his/her job.

I was shocked both by the allegations and by the fact that the city wasn't investigating them. I was so shocked by the city's lack of reaction, that I immediately filed a citizen's complaint against the Chief of Police, as was my right, but I didn't send it to the Mayor. Instead, I sent my complaint to the City Attorney, telling him the City had a duty to investigate these claims under city policy. Thankfully, the City Attorney called me. He offered to have a neutral person investigate the allegations, and we agreed upon a prominent local attorney in an adjoining city to do so.

That attorney was to set up a confidential process which would allow police officers or citizens to speak with him confidentially. The city and this attorney made a public statement that the claims were being taken seriously, that an investigation was being opened, and that the results of that investigation would be made public upon its conclusion.

The problem is, the process wasn't confidential nor would they follow through with their promise of making the findings public. The police Chief ensured loyal officers camped outside this attorney's office or in the attorney's lobby to see who was speaking with this attorney. Their presence certainly acted as a deterrent. When I complained, I was told they were delivering materials for the attorney to consider.

My confidential source and I then set up a time to meet with this attorney, supposedly in confidence, but when we showed up, a uniformed officer just happened to be sitting in the lobby. I expressed my dissatisfaction to this attorney. To my dismay, this attorney didn't seem to care about the lack of confidentiality, and in fact, seemed to take the Chief's side that this KKK coin was simply a piece of evidence recovered from an old crime scene that he was proud to carry because he did the public a bit of good in putting this bad guy away. A piece of evidence? What was the crime? When? Who was this unknown bad guy? The story smelled. If that story was true, why hadn't the Chief ever told this story before? Why hadn't he told it when showing the coin to police officers on duty? What wreaked even more was the fact that a police chief in this modern day and era was carrying a KKK coin and showing it. He was either too stupid to be a police chief, a member of the KKK, or both.

The attorney eventually finished his investigation, but failed to make his findings public as promised citing attorney client privilege. Importantly, part of the report was sent from the city to a Federal agency investigating a complaint of Veteran discrimination, also one of the anonymous allegations. I had a copy of that fax and the portion of the report concerning Veterans, though I didn't have the full report concerning the KKK allegations. I filed a freedom of information act request for the full report. The city and the attorney objected to producing it on the grounds that it was an attorney client privileged investigation exempt from FOI. I filed suit and we went to court.

On the stand, the smug attorney, "my senior" in years of practice, admitted he was properly quoted in the news when he said that his findings would be made public, but testified that his client now instructed him not to make the findings public. When I asked if a client could waive attorney client privilege, he admitted they could. When I asked if the client sent the report to someone else, would that waive the privilege, he admitted it could. I then showed him the portion of his report concerning Veteran discrimination, and he admitted it was from his report. When I asked how I had a copy of that portion of his report, he said he didn't know, and when confronted with the fax page, he admitted it came from the city. The judge found that by producing a portion of the report the city waived the privilege and ordered the entire report produced, and the Chief of Police resigned the next day.

My anonymous officer then told me to be careful. He said that the former Chief was furious, dangerous, and told me what his civilian car looked like, and that if I ever saw it at my house or following me, to call him and the police immediately. I never had to.

The Hispanic Abuse that Didn't Happened

The Bible says that the tongue sets the world on fire, and thus fake news runs like wildfire through our city streets scorching everything and everyone in its path. Many years ago, I helplessly watched fake news burn my brother, almost to death, in the city streets of Nashville, Tennessee. He was a police officer caught up in an unfortunate political maelstrom without an eye for any political respite. Nashville is the home of the Grand Ole Opry, a city which hides its sins behind the smile of its big bosomed saint, Dolly Parton. Do not be deceived, though, by the bright lights and fake smiles.

It all began when a local reporter looking for a story created a fake one, full of virulent hyperbole that white police officers, working off duty security, were abusing Hispanic residents at a local apartment complex, a serious allegation if true, but he offered no facts to support it, only inflammatory descriptors like white police officers abusing Hispanics off duty. Only one officer was named by name in the article, and my brother wasn't that officer. It also didn't say what the "abuse" was, when it was done, or quote any sources, but it started a political fire which smolders to this day in the hearts of the three police officers burned beyond description, but who somehow managed to survive.

The article generated a public outcry, and to appease the masses, the black police chief began a public witch hunt, an internal investigation, and put three suspected witches, three white police officers on "administrative desk duty" pending the completion of his investigation. My brother was one of those three officers. None of the three public "suspects" had any disciplinary history. In fact, their records were exemplary. One of them had just been named the national police officer of the year. I had a photo of then President Bill Clinton putting a medal around his neck.

Despite their exemplary records, and despite the fact that no one had accused them of wrongdoing, the state attorney general also opened an investigation to appease the masses but found no wrongdoing and closed his file, but this wasn't enough for the Chief to return them to duty. The Federal Department of Justice also opened an investigation, found nothing wrong and also closed their file, but this didn't satisfy the Chief either, who kept the three officers on desk duty, as if he knew something the others didn't, and in so doing, continued to publicly impugn their exemplary reputations.

My father talked to the Chief, in person, and the Chief refused to put a time table on their being restored to full duty. He continued to castigate them both publicly and within the department by forcing them to work at the front desk of the police department, in civilian clothes, for every citizen and every police officer to see. This public humiliation was hard on officers charged with no wrongdoing other than an unsubstantiated article. These men were all married, two of them had kids at home, the stress on them and their families was tremendous. The constant being held out as a political scapegoat was almost unbearable. My brother would end up divorced as a result of this.

Something needed to be done. These men needed help, needed justice where none was offered. If there was to be a trial, then let them be tried in court with evidence, and not in the court of public opinion. We demanded their day in court, to face whatever charges of wrongdoing they may bring, but they played chess and refused to bring charges.

We began our counter-assault by filing an EEOC complaint alleging racial discrimination by a black police chief against three white officers, who had not been accused of wrongdoing, where no victim ever came forward. There were plenty of cases where black officers were accused of wrongdoing, where victims had been named, but those black officers had never been stripped of the vestiges of their position and were at least afforded the opportunity to face charges. So, why were these three white officers being treated differently? The EEOC complaint would force the Chief and City of Nashville to give reasons why.

Simultaneously, we filed a civil rights law suit to force the Chief to produce the department's supposed internal investigation file into the news article's allegations. The suit alleged that their being stripped of police duties violated their civil service status without a due process - the right to a hearing. It was a case of first impression, as they continued at the same pay, just not with the outward vestiges of their position.

The Chief refused to produce his file, but the trial judge finally ordered it to be produced. It was produced and to my relief, the Chief didn't have any cards hidden up his sleeve. It was a big nothing burger. No victims had ever been found nor any complaint against these three officers ever been made.

So why did the Chief pick on these three officers? It became more nefarious than the news article. Two of these officers used to work a plains clothes detail for the Chief, a five-man detail personally pulling drug dealers out of their cars in high-risk stops. They knew a lot about the Chief and the dark inner machinations of Nashville politics, organized crime, and how people in the police department were used in all of this. They suspected they knew too much, and were being pushed out because of what they knew, not because of the article.

What did they know? They told me what I didn't know, but what made complete sense after they told me. Nefarious entities were using the police department to carry on their illegal activities in the city. What I learned was that to control a police department, there are only two people in the police department that need be "on the payroll." Those two people are the chief and the lead homicide detective. Those two positions control everything else. They control what gets investigated, what gets over looked, and if investigated, who investigates it.

Even if true, how could I prove it? The starting point was the lead homicide detective's car. Each year he bought a brand-new Mercedes for cash. They told me the type, and the type of car he bought for cash was more than his yearly salary. They drove me by his house to see, and there it was, exactly the car they said, and he owed nothing on it. As for the Chief, harder to prove, but they knew of a local "security company", a front company for all kinds of illegal activity, like running gambling money through the city. They said this security company had often paid the Chief cash "off the books" for off-duty "security" work of his own. Once, they made the mistake of handing him a check and not paying him in cash. So, I subpoenaed a copy of their check to the Chief.

When I went to pick up the check, a big muscled up guy met me in his office. He looked like a testosterone filled professional wrestler, but he wasn't fake, he was real, and he was real interested in me and why I wanted that check. He towered over me and reached out to shake my hand with one hand and held out the check with his other. When I shook his hand and grasped the check, he didn't let go of either the check or my hand. Instead, he looked down and asked:

"Hey little man, you're a long way from home, aren't you?"

"Not that far," I said. "Less than a day's drive."

"Do you worry about leaving your wife and kids at home."

He obviously knew more about me than I knew about him. He wasn't inquiring about them, but threatening them.

"No, I'm not worried" I tried to feign. "We have a good police department."

He continued to hold my hand in his, and also the check. Then he asked, "What do you want with this check?"

"I don't really want this check."

"Then what do you want?"

"Do you see those three men in your lobby?" My brother and the other two officers were in his lobby. "One of those men is my brother, and all I want is for him to have his uniform back on. And as soon as that happens, however that happens, I'm going home."

He handed me the check and we left.

But this was only scratching the surface, for I knew that a local armored car company was owned by some of these corrupt higher-ranking officers and used to move illegal gambling money throughout the city. Who would ever stop an armored car? Especially armored cars owned and operated by a fellow high-ranking police officer?

I sent discovery to these armored car companies, asking for ownership information and other information needed to prove my case, but I would never get that information. The day before the deadline for the other third-parties to produce this information, the judge, without motion of any of the parties, dismissed my case for failure to state a cause of action. It is extremely unusual for a judge to dismiss a lawsuit without a motion by a party to do so. In fact, I had never heard of a judge doing that and there was legal question if he could. He also ordered me to pay all the defendants attorney's fees, a sizeable sum.

We appealed. On appeal, in an unpublished opinion, the Federal Court ruled that, though unusual, the judge had the inherent authority to dismiss the case on his own, that since my clients had not officially been charged or disciplined, they had no right to a due process hearing, but reversed the ruling ordering me to pay attorney fees.

The city then brought administrative charges of wrongdoing against my clients, over 100 pages. My clients were administered a polygraph and passed. We beat all those vague charges, because there was no merit, and the acting administrative judge ordered the three officers returned to full duty status immediately. It was a great day for my clients to walk into the sunshine after that hearing, surrounded by reporters, innocent of the heinous unfounded allegations, but the damage had been done. Only one of the officers would remain with the Nashville police department. My brother and another left, and a few years later, my brother got divorced.

The EEOC would later rule that a black police Chief discriminated against three white officers, but the reporter that started this political witch hunt never ran that story, as it's not the kind of justice the public demands, nor would he ever report how the police Chief would retire much earlier than anyone expected.

In the end, there was no "justice" in this case, not the way that the public views justice, where three falsely accused police officers retire with a big settlement at the end. It ended with three good officers returned to duty, bruised and battered, after fighting over a year to clear their name, and with me writing so many years later, still trying to clear my lungs from the smoke inhaled at that time, coughing about an injustice that wasn't undone.

The Cross Examination of the Credible Mr. Reed

Mr. Reed was a former college football player. He was tall, dark, handsome, smart and charismatic. After college, he took all he learned in school along with his God given talents and became an appraiser, a very successful one.

Mr. Reed was as dangerous and charismatic in the field of appraising as he was on the gridiron. He quickly developed a reputation as an expert witness in the courtroom on land condemnation suits. No other appraiser could compete against the soft spoken charisma of Mr. Reed. If the numbers where in dispute, his innate charisma could be counted on to carry the day. It wasn't long before every government body condemning property hired Mr. Reed before a landowner could.

My Dad was a local attorney and longtime friend of Mr. Reed. Their friendship went back years and each shared a mutual respect and admiration for the other. But in the courtroom, my Dad had his job and Mr. Reed had his. Mr. Reed's job was to testify for the State and my Dad's was to cross examine him on behalf of the landowner. My job? I was a young lawyer who had yet to ask a question in court. So my job was to sit and take notes. These are my notes.

When the State finished examining Mr. Reed, I was thoroughly convinced he was right. Had I been taken in by his charm? Maybe, but in the end it was all about the numbers and his added up in a way I could understand.

It was my Dad's turn to cross examine the credible Mr. Reed. My Dad had a habit of allowing a little time to pass before beginning his cross examination. Most people abhor the pressure of public speaking, but good trial attorneys must embrace it and cannot be distracted by the pressure of all the eyes studying their every move. A good trial attorney must enter that arena like they are fighting a bull and never take their eyes off the bull. My Dad stood before the credible Mr. Reed like a Matador. I didn't envy the position he was in, having to throw stones at this courtroom Goliath.

Where would my Dad begin? What would be his first question? How would he attack the credibility of a man he loved more than the jury? The surprise? He wouldn't, because it couldn't be done. What he would do instead is turn the credible Mr. Reed into a witness of his own. Use the credible Mr. Reed to testify as to the credibility our meek, wobbly kneed expert appraiser, Mr. Smith. And by using Mr. Reed to testify to both the credibility and numbers used by Mr. Smith, he would cut off the other attorney's attack, because attacking Smith would essentially be attacking the opinion of their own witness, the credible Mr. Reed.

Q = Question and A = Answer of Mr. Reed.

My Dad began:

Q: Mr. Reed, do you recognize the man sitting in the back of the courtroom (My Dad pointed to Mr. Smith)?

A: Yes.

Q: Who is he?

A: That's Mr. Smith.

Q: How do you know him?

A: I know him professionally, as an appraiser.

Q: How long have you known him?

A: At least fifteen years.

Q: Please describe the professional relationship you've had over those years?

A: During those years, we've served on various committees together.

Q: Was one of those committees the ethics committee?

A. Yes.

Q: Do you serve together on the ethics committee now?

A: Yes.

Q: What does the ethics committee do?

A: We investigate complaints that appraisers are not acting ethically in the way that they do appraisals.

Q: What is an example of that?

A: Sometimes there are complaints that an appraiser has not used proper comparable sales data or maybe not used a proper formula for calculating the value of a property.

Q: Has Mr. Smith ever had a complaint filed against him?

A: Not that I'm aware of.

Q: Are you aware that Mr. Smith did an appraisal of the property in this case?

A: Yes.

Q: Have you read that appraisal?

A. Yes.

Q: In this case, has anyone complained that Mr. Smith's appraisal violates the accepted methods for appraising property in the State of Arkansas?

A: No.

Q: Are you familiar with the comparable sales data used by Mr. Smith?

A: Yes.

Q: Are you also familiar with the formula Mr. Smith used to value this property?

A: Yes.

Q: Appraisers are allowed discretion when choosing comparable sales?

A: Some.

Q: And Mr. Smith's comparable sales are acceptable.

A. Yes but not the ones I would choose.

Q: Is there any suggestion that Mr. Smith's sales data is improper?

A: No.

Q: So the two of you, in picking sales data, properly used your discretion in picking comparable sales data?

A: Yes.

Q: And the properties used by both of you are acceptable under State of Arkansas appraisal standards?

A: Yes.

Q: Also Mr. Smith used a different formula to calculate value the property?

A: Yes.

Q: Mr. Smith's formula is an accepted valuation method?

A: Yes, but not the one I believe should be used.

Q: But it's an accepted method for valuing property that he has the discretion to use?

A: Yes.

Q: And the end result is that your formula gives a lower value than his?

A: Yes.

Q: So when you combine your sales data with your formula, it will always end up with a lower value than his sales data with his formula?

A: Yes.

Q: When you read Mr. Smith's appraisal and review the sales data with the formula he used, is his final number correct? Did his math add up?

A: Yes.

Q: No further questions for Mr. Reed.

Not once did my Dad attempt to cross examine the credible Mr. Reed on the values he used or the formula he used. That's a dangerous fight my Dad couldn't have won. Instead, he artfully used Mr. Reed's credibility to build the credibility of Mr. Smith. By using Mr. Reed's credibility instead of attacking it, it made it next to impossible for the other side to cross examine Mr. Smith, for Mr. Reed just told the jury that Mr. Smith was a credible appraiser he had known for fifteen years who properly used his discretion in this case.

The only question remaining for the jury was who's final number should they believe? Mr. Reed's or Mr. Smith's? By using the credibility of Mr. Reed to build the credibility of Mr. Smith, my Dad essentially put the two experts on par. Putting them on par shifted the issue of credibility from who had the most credible expert to who had the most credible attorney? It was now up to the attorneys to persuade the jurors whose number they should use.

After closing arguments, it didn't take long for the jury to return a verdict using Mr. Smith's number.

Meaning

Over the last several days, I thought about the meaning of my Father's life. It seems lives have meaning and I wanted to take some meaning from my Father's life and wrap it up at his service today. In reflecting on his life, one thing stood out: he was born poor but accomplished many things due to the help of many people along the way. If there's a lesson to be drawn from my Father's life it is this: if you change the life of a child, you change the world, and not just the child's world, but the world we live in and your future too.

My Father was born into an almost incomprehensible poverty, born in dusty Western Oklahoma during the Great Depression, into a home without running water or electricity, but still somehow went to college, became an attorney, a State Senator, a happily married man of 55 years, a father and grandfather. How does that happen? It only happens when a kid gets help. This isn't a sink or swim world for kids. We don't throw a kid in the deep end of life and expect him or her to survive. Kids have to be taught to swim to the edge and climb out of their circumstance.

One time, in a quiet moment at our office, my Father looked at me and said "Chris, I've spent my entire life trying to repay everyone that helped me along the way, but one lifetime won't be enough." We sit here today and see everything he became, but what my Father remembered were the "make me or break me" moments along that hard road to success, moments when he didn't break only because of the helping hands of people that cared enough to reach out, and help a poor boy in the deep end of life swim to the edge and pull himself out of his circumstance.

One of those people was his high school teacher Mr. Sutton, now deceased. Before my Father graduated, Mr. Sutton asked my Father what his plans were after high school. My Father didn't have any. My Father's Father was a hard-working farmer with a third-grade education, unable to give my Father a vision of anything beyond the farm. At the time, my Father was living in a house without running water or electricity.

Mr. Sutton gave my Father a vision of a world beyond the farm and asked if he thought of college, but my Father hadn't. Mr. Sutton took my Father on a tour of the University of Arkansas campus and when that tour was over asked if my Father would like to enroll. My Father saw only obstacles. He said he didn't have the money, because he didn't have the money. Mr. Sutton took that obstacle away and offered to pay his first semester if my Father would enroll. In making that offer, Mr. Sutton threw my father a life line out of the pool of poverty. My Father said yes and Mr. Sutton paid his first semester. Though Mr. Sutton is deceased, we stand in gratitude to his family to whom we remain forever close.

My Father didn't have the money to continue college and joined the Army. He wanted to be the best, so he became a paratrooper, and while in service, got married and had a son. When he was discharged, he returned to this vision of finishing college. The Army wasn't as good then as it is now about paying for school, so my Father worked full time to pay for his school and support his wife and child. That's not easy to do.

By the time my Father got to law school, he was tired and broke, tired from working the night shift in a chicken plant and too broke with his low paying job to feed his family and also buy his school books. As any good father would do, he chose to feed his family and forego buying his books. The Dean of his law school saw my Father register but not buy his books. The Dean bought my Father's law books for him. My Father said he didn't know when he could repay him. The Dean said don't repay me, just do the same for someone else someday. Now, we call that "paying it forward." To the Dean, we are forever thankful.

My Father finished law school, but the law degree doesn't allow you to practice law. You still have to pass a comprehensive test called the Bar Exam. It takes a lot of study time to pass this exam, time that my Father, working in the chicken plant to put food on the table, didn't have. This was a breaking point for a young father. My father had a family to feed and couldn't quit work to study, and this dream he had of becoming a lawyer began to fade away.

He cried that night under the pressure of life. He was in the deep end and saw no way out of his circumstance. He needed a lifeline. My mother saw her young paratrooper crying. She was powerless to help and said a prayer. Their fate was out of their hands and now in God's.

The next morning, God knocked on their door. Standing at the door were the Trinkle sisters from Huntsville, Arkansas. They were wearing their home-made dresses. They had little money, but the little they had they were saving for someone in need, and their prayers led them to "Little Johnny" an old Huntsville friend trying to work his way through school. With that money, my Father was able to quit working at the chicken plant and study for the Bar Exam. He passed the Bar exam with the highest score and became a lawyer. My Father could never talk about the Trinkle sisters without crying.

My Father spent the remainder of his life trying to repay all the people who helped him along the way, by paying it forward. We had a case one time, where a commercial truck crossed the center line and struck a car head on, killing a young mother, father, and two children. One child survived, an infant in a car seat. It's the type of case where an attorney can make a lot of money. My father didn't. When all was said and done, he waived all fees and expenses and told me that baby boy needed the money more than we did. My Father saw himself in the face of every child he met. He loved them all.

I wonder, as we sit here today, how many other "Little Johnnies," how many "John Lisle's" are out there living as children in poverty waiting for their opportunity to be great. Our world, our future, needs more John Lisle's as Fathers, needs more John Lisle's as husbands that love their spouse through thick and thin for 55 years, our world needs more John Lisle's as attorneys, needs more John Lisle's as political leaders, needs more John Lisle's as paratroopers protecting our country. The future "Little Johnnies" are out there if you will only look for them.

Look for them in the face of every child you meet, and if you change their lives, you no longer have to worry about your future, for if you change the life of every child you meet, you change the future of your world and their world forever. Blessed are the children.

"The Cop"

Good people will do what they find honourable to do, even if it requires hard work and causes them injury."
Seneca, Moral Letters, 76.18

Four days ago, his first call of the day was a suicide. A mother went to get her fourteen-year-old boy up for school and found him hanging in his bedroom. The wails of a despondent mother are hard to forget, impossible to forget he told me, but it wasn't the first time he heard someone scream like that. Three days later, Sunday morning at 10 am, I stood beside him as he did CPR on an 87-year-old man who had fallen on his driveway. His head lay in a large pool of blood.

"Springdale 123" is a Police Officer. "Springdale 123" is his radio call sign, but he's more than a number called out over the radio. He is a 53-year-old, tall, Hispanic police officer, a patrol sergeant, still working the streets after 25 years of service. He is my friend. His name is Robert Sanchez.

We were first on the scene and I watched "Springdale 123" on his knees doing CPR until the ambulance arrived. It seemed to take forever for the ambulance to get there, but it couldn't have been more than a few minutes. "Springdale 123" said he had done CPR many times before, but it was always too late he sighed, but he always tried. He tried again today as the despondent family members looked on and cried uncontrollably. I hope it did some good today. I don't know.

I've been friends with "Springdale 123" since I was six years old. We met at a baseball game. I was eating a corn dog. My Dad was in the dugout coaching a baseball team that our older brothers played on. Six-year-old "Springdale 123" stood outside the dugout fence and asked my Dad if he could spend the night. My Dad said he couldn't but thought I could. That struck up a friendship that lasted all through grade school, all through high school, through the Army together as paratroopers, and now through this morning as I watched him do CPR on an 87-year-old Korean War Vet that fell, I suspect, for the last time.

I was riding with "Springdale 123" today. It's not the first time I've ridden with him and won't be the last. I once rode with him and we ended up on a hot pursuit chasing a guy in a pickup holding a gun to his girlfriend's head. We were the first police car in a line of police cars but got nailed by a truck that T-Boned us going through an intersection. We were lucky to survive. The police car didn't.

Today, the biggest thing on "Springdale 123"'s mind is a local bad guy. "Springdale 123" and the rest of his officers are on the lookout for a real bad guy, not just some guy pissed off at his girlfriend, but a guy with a long dangerous history of robbery, drugs, fighting and running from the police, a bad guy on a tear lately running through the city evading the police. "Springdale 123" knows if they find him, he will run again, not because he is scared of the police, but because he thinks like Bonnie and Clyde. He will run until he can't and then he will fight. In twenty-five years "Springdale 123" has seen a lot of bad guys, and this one stands out. "Springdale 123" is worried about his guys, younger officers without twenty-five years' experience.

This is liable to be a long day, and at our age, we have to make sure we go to the bathroom before we hit the streets. The ladies at the gas station where we stop all know "Springdale 123" by his first name. You can see their faces warm when he walks in and says "Hi." He takes a moment to see how they are doing and make sure everything is OK.

We leave the station, and as we get back into the police car, he gets serious again. It's the same look he got when talking about the bad guy on his mind. He knows they will eventually find him, he's just not sure when, but any day could be the day. He looks at me and says, "You don't have to go with me today."

"What are you saying?" I ask.

"You have a wife and kids at home. That's all" he says.

He loves me and he's worried about me getting hurt. And I love him too. I hope he knows that.

"Well you got a wife and kids at home too" I said.

He smiled. "Yes, I do."

Death of a Poor Man

Matthew Noble died last night in his sleep. He was my friend. We met back in about 2004 when he began renting a small farm house from me. He lived there ever since, and that's where he passed away, on a small farm that he loved. He loved the apples that grew on the old apple tree in the front yard. He grew a few other things around the house like peppers and tomatoes which he always shared, and he didn't have much to share, for by any measure of the wallet, he was a poor man, but he loved life in a way that I never could, and loved God in a way that I always should.

Matthew had a beautiful six-year-old daughter that he loved more than life. He was a wonderful father. There aren't many fathers or people in this world like Matthew Noble.

When Julie called me with the news that Matthew passed away, it made me sad. I loved the time we shared together. He said he talked too much, but I never thought so, because while he was talking too much, he always thanked me for my friendship. It made me feel special. Thank you for your friendship Matthew. I will miss you. I already do.

As a post script I would add, that in these tragic times when we ask ourselves why are some men so bad, this was one man that should cause us to ask, why are some men so good?

Matthew Scott, He lived a Good Story

"Life is like a play: it's not the length, but the excellence of the acting that matters."
Seneca

(Matthew Scott, Iraq, Gulf War I)

High on an Alaskan glacier, a young Army Lieutenant led a small mountaineering party up an icy ridge, slowly ascending the treacherous glacial slope. For reasons unknown, two West Point Cadets on that climb unhooked from their safety rope and fell off the edge of that icy ridge, falling to their deaths into a deep ravine over 100 feet below. That was over twenty years ago, and that "young" Army Lieutenant is now my friend, and he still remembers the names of those two young cadets, the moment he saw them sliding over the edge, and the long climb down to recover their bodies encapsulated at the bottom of an icy grave.

Life is not that kind, and unfortunately tragedy did not end at the bottom of that that icy Alaskan ravine. My friend would go on to witness the fiery deaths of over twenty paratroopers at Ft. Bragg, North Carolina. That young Lieutenant would later become a Captain, serving as a paratrooper in the infamous 82nd Airborne Division. As luck would have it, or was it fate, he was on the runway when a fighter plane crashed into hundreds of paratroopers boarding planes for a parachute jump. Some paratroopers were already sitting on the planes and all were killed. Others, like him, were inside a large hanger putting on their parachutes when the building was suddenly and unexpectedly rocked by a large explosion and engulfed with fire. He stood in that hanger and watched the fireball consume the paratroopers in it. He can still see those men burning and smell the burning of their flesh. The thought of it churns his stomach and he chases it away with a swig of beer at our favorite pub, The Odd Soul.

The man in the pink sport coat. No one goes to war in a pink sport coat, so when my friend stumbled upon a dying Iraqi soldier wearing one, it moved him then and now to tears. The dying man was holding a photo of himself at a wedding, wearing that same pink sport coat. The coat he wore today was thus a special coat he put on for special occasions, and on this day, he put it on knowing it would be his last, thus the most special day of all his days, as special as his birth. And he carried with him, on his last day, a photo which gave meaning to all the days of his life in between its beginning and its end. And as the man died, my friend held him and tried his best to comfort him in those most important final moments of the dying man's life.

And now my friend wonders about his life. He told me that one day, as a soldier, he would be buried in the national cemetery. All the military would allow on his tombstone would be his name and rank, but if they would allow more, he would have them write a short epitaph saying "He lived a good story." "Good" I think to myself. Is my friend not sure he is good? And then he digresses in thought, because he says even that is not enough, for a story can be so many things, a tragedy, comedy, drama, so what kind of story did he live and more importantly, did his life story impact anyone?

I have an advantage over my friend, an advantage that all friends have over friends, the advantage of being able to look into his eyes and into a soul which God has forbidden him from seeing, for no man can look into their own eyes and is thus forever forbidden from seeing his own soul. I see his story is far more than standing on an icy mountain, or standing in a fiery hanger, or holding a dying Iraqi man, for he is also the father of three children, and to hear him recount the births of his children and hear the impact of holding them for the first time, looking into their eyes and hearing their cries, I see the heart of a good man whose children carved his soul just as deeply as descending into an icy ravine to recover the bodies of the dead. He has been married for thirty-five years, he reads every day, and once set a goal to read over 300 books in one year, which he did. He has tasted financial success but also tasted its defeat. Inside the facade of any man beats a heart, and the heart of this man once told me that he wants to finish his life with as few regrets as possible. Like all good men, the mistakes of his life are carved into the marble of his soul, giving it form.

As I look into his gentle eyes and bear witness to the hash marks of regret carved into the mountain of his soul, I tell him that his is the Biblical story of Adam, and Adam is the story of us all, for we are all born into this world innocent, but all eventually take a bite of the apple and leave the innocent bosoms of our mothers. If we are lucky, we fall in love and marry, just as Adam did, and have families of our own, none of which are perfect. And with each honest life, there are honest regrets living it, and those regrets cause us to stumble, but in stumbling, we look to the ground beneath our feet and find meaning hidden in places we couldn't see before we fell. And on this night, this pub where we sit is full of Adams, some toasting their friends, others drowning their sorrows, but Adams we all are, and far from grace we have all fallen, but thankfully into the waiting arms of each other.

And whether in happiness or sorry, we know that all things must end, and in the end, it doesn't matter what epitaph they write on your grave, for no gravestone will be large enough to write the story of you my friend, so deeply carved into my soul. But neither I nor any friend needs your story written on your grave when it is already written so deeply into our hearts. All I need to see or hear is your name to open the story of a friendship – a whale of a tale, as big as Adam's, and if God won't offer you his forgiveness, then I will.

Adam Bain, the Weary Gentleman

An empty heart is the worst form of poverty

Adam Bain is a changed man, changed by war. But who isn't? If you weren't crazy going in, you are crazy coming out, but I didn't know Adam before the war, so I don't know if Adam was driven crazy by the war or a weird example of a traumatic brain injury turning someone into a mad genius rather than a potato.

Adam somehow survived an IED blast, suffering a debilitating head injury for which he will forever be medicated. The medicine isn't enough to assuage the pain, so he smokes cigarettes and pounds whiskey all night with a pistol on the table and a laptop nearby.

Adam fights a perpetual war that is no longer on the news, a war that no one else is fighting except men like him who will forever be stuck in that desert and cannot return home. For the survivors, it is a war that cannot be won. Dick Cheney, who sent boys like Adam to that war, recently got a new heart and a new lease on life, but there are no new brains for guys like Adam. Adam will live the rest of his life with the memory of a war that ends each night with cigarettes, whiskey, and a pistol.

So far, Adam hasn't put the pistol to his head and pulled the trigger, maybe because he has a young daughter by a failed marriage. She doesn't see him the way we do, not yet. She is too young to see anything but her Daddy. But when that changes, will he pull the trigger?

At any rate, and for whatever reason, Adam keeps on drinking at night and pounding the laptop espousing truths that can only found at the bottom of a whiskey bottle, truths only spoken by a person so low in life they don't care what you think and speak with an honesty so painful it's not tolerated in a polite company.

After pounding enough whiskey, Adams turns to pounding the keyboard like a drunken Earnest Hemmingway and posts his writings under the penname "The Weary Gentleman." You should check his writing out in case he decides to check out. Now, you and I know that checking out doesn't end his pain, it only spreads it around to his surviving brothers at arms, forcing them to deal with yet another casualty of a war that cannot be won.

In our conversations, Adam is constantly driven crazy by the realization he was dumb enough to believe the U.S. Government when it said the Iraqis had "weapons of mass destruction", aka nuclear bombs, and were going to end us all in a mushroom cloud if we didn't go to war and stop them. Remember being told that? Adam does. He believed them and volunteered to go to war to save our country even if it meant life or limb. He gave a little of both.

The problem is, our government lied about all that, and no one cares but the guys that paid the price for the lie. Adam kicks himself in the ass for believing what I believed too. The difference is, Adam suffers for his belief. I don't. And no one but the guys like Adam really care about that lie anymore. Like Adam slamming whiskey into the night, the lie is forgotten and no longer a part of our political discourse.

Adam wasn't any dumber than his forefathers. The political elite never fight the wars but always manage to get poor slobs to do the dirty work for them, and when the poor slobs like Adam return, they give them shiny little $5 purple hearts that get lost in a sock drawer or forgotten in a bottle.

The age old process of the elite lying to get men to fight was best expressed by the infamous Nazi Hermann Goering who said "Why would some poor slob on a farm want to risk his life in a war when the best he can get out of it is to come back in one piece . . .the people can always be brought to the bidding of the leaders. That is easy. All you have to do is tell them they are being attacked, and denounce the peace makers for lack of patriotism and exposing the country to danger. It works the same in any country." Goering gave us the elite Nazi playbook a generation ago and every sitting U.S. President since then has followed it and used patriotic lies to send poor boys to fight in hellholes we call Vietnam, Grenada, Panama, and finally to fight mushroom clouds in Iraq.

Why lie to go to war? Politics is big business. War is big business. The only way to increase business is increasing political market through war. We are in the business of war and poor slobs like Adam are the physical capital who pay the ultimate price to increase someone else's bottom line.

Adam is tortured now with the realization he got his head blown up fighting a war against people he thought had nuclear bombs but didn't. The only thing he discovered in the desert of Iraq were poor people barely out of the stone age with arcane perverted notions of God, as arcane and perverted as ours. The God preached here is a loving God, as refreshing as the cool AC in the summer. If you give enough money, he will fix your AC, maybe even win your Friday night football game. The God preached there is as heartless and ruthless as the unforgiving poverty and heat of the desert. In neither country, though, has God ended the suffering of war. As Plato said, only the dead have seen the end of war.

Adam is still waiting on God to end his war, either the God of the desert or God of the land from sea to shining sea. It doesn't matter which one comes. Until then, he pounds his whiskey and pounds his laptop writing as Weary Gentleman.

Still a Boy

After my father passed, there was an hour or so when I thought I was finally a man, at least forced to become a man, because I had no father left to run to. But after about a day or so, I wondered if that was true. It seems I was still running to him, running to him in my mind. I couldn't quit thinking of him like he was still here. I thought of him as often as I did when he was here. There was not that emptiness in my heart that I expected. He was still there, in my heart, just like always.

He hadn't left. I remembered walking down Emma Street with him when I was maybe five, or waiting for him to come home from work to tell him I ate all his supper, just to hear him play like he was mad. I could still see him reading a book, in fact, I still have his books. Some of my books are mixed with his books, and some of his with mine. We haven't returned them to each other yet, and I don't see the hurry. Having grown up with him and having worked with him as a lawyer for almost twenty years, I think we talked about almost everything under the sun, and I haven't forgotten any of it. Over the years, since we had talked about everything already, we often didn't talk, we just sat and enjoyed each other's company. And it seems we are still doing that now. I am still sitting and enjoying his company, just like I always did. So, I was wrong. I never became a man. I am still that boy, my father's boy, still sitting on his knee or telling him my night time prayers, trying a case with him, reading his books and listening to his words that guide me still, and eating all his supper. He's going to be mad.

The Story of David

David was God's favorite. I never knew the David of the Bible, only read about him. But if he was anything like the David I know; I know why God loved him.

David was one of my Father's favorites too. David was an architect, but he had also been a soldier, a soldier that returned home from the Vietnam War in 1968. As a young boy, I remember walking in one night when my Dad and David were in a deep conversation about that war. David had only been home a couple of years at most, but the war was still going on in Vietnam and inside of David. I was too young to understand anything of what was said, but of the love of my Father for David, I did understand.

After my father passed, I was blessed that David continued a friendship with me, but much more than a friendship, as he is as close to a father figure as I could hope for now that my Father is gone, one that I still need, and one which my own Father would desire me to have.

Not so long ago, I found myself having that same conversation with David that my Father had so many years ago, one that I couldn't understand then, and still can't understand now, because I wasn't in Vietnam, but hoped in hearing about his experience I could better understand how it shaped the man that I came to love as a surrogate father.

During that conversation, David mentioned that he had kept a journal during that war. Journals reflect the heart of a thinking man, and David was a thinking man, a man whose heart was sewn as a boy born in small town Arkansas, seeded by a father who was a minister, who aptly named him David. Little did David know his name would prove to be a divinely inspired gift from father to son, to guide a son through times of darkness, a constant daily reminder that with David's faith in God, one could remain on the right path even when that path was shrouded with darkness.

And life would turn dark for David in Vietnam. "There are many stories of desecration of bodies here in Vietnam. Last week, four

VC were killed and another captured. The heads of the dead were cut off and strung by wire on a bamboo pole and the captured men made to carry the heads of the dead up and down a village street. Do men become animals? Or are all men the same in war?"

This was David's fear, that he would be changed by war. "I wonder if my attitude and character will change? .... "Some conditions tend to make deep impressions on me ... It must be this kind of thinking that causes poets to write and singers sing. How will I be affected?"

"I hope the war ends soon" he wrote. "So many people are getting killed." Throughout the trying year, David constantly longed to return home to his young 22 y/o wife and new born daughter, whom he only knew through pictures. "I didn't realize the closeness and dependence I had experienced with L*** until now. It must be a miracle to love; and to appreciate. My daughter is perfect. God was generous and overfilled our lives with that little thing ... I pray God to help my wife during this year."

His diary reflects a young Army Officer, husband, a father and Christian, struggling inside to understand war. "I wonder what God thinks of this human invention of destruction. War seems to be anti-everything. The death and misery caused must equal all the torment of hell ... Will God wait?" 1-14 68. "I wonder if the Vietnam will ever have peace. These people live in fear. They all have bunkers and barbed wire fences. Their simple culture is being confused by the ways of war. Their values are changing. Will they ever be corrected?"

After seventeen civilians were blown up by a mine, and five wounded, David wrote "God must be watching my life. This is one of those times when nothing can take your mind from the tragedy of today. My thoughts turned to hopeless thoughts about mankind and his inability to live with himself. I hope I can gain some benefit from this experience." 3-27-68.

While David's thoughts turned hopeless about Vietnam surviving the war, his hope for our country also waned. The news from home was equally as hopeless. Riots protesting the war rocked our nation's core and David questioned our country's future with the assassinations of Bobby Kennedy and Martin Luther King.

On April 5, 1968, he recorded "Martin Luther King died of a gunshot wound today. I understand that riots are in some of the major cities." On June 6, 1958 he recorded "Yesterday, Robert Kennedy was shot. Today he died. What can be said for America. I wonder what the people of the world must think of America. There is such a void in our society. Will it be filled in my lifetime?"

Despite his deep questions and occasional thoughts of hopelessness for mankind, his diary continually logged his attendance at church, his Easter in Vietnam, and that God had spared him of the death around him.

In reading this journal, we know what young David doesn't know at that time. That the war would one day end, and that he would return home to his wife and have not just one beautiful daughter, but three. So how will he be judged? Not judged by you or me, but by God? Did he turn into the feared animal of war that corrupted so many others?

Matthew 25 says that God will judge David by how he treated his fellow man, whether he clothed the poor, fed the hungry, and helped his fellow man in need. Even in all the darkness of war, as David the warrior of the Bible built Jerusalem for God, David the soldier and architect, David the Army engineer, built schools, bridges, and dug wells for farmers in Vietnam, and David the father, far away from his own baby daughter, noted a moment of joy being allowed to administer medicine to a sick sleeping infant. "I helped the medic give pills and give a liquid to infants. One child, about a month old was asleep. I put the liquid just a little at a time in its mouth; it began to suck and took all the medicine without waking." 1-9-68.

He was so beloved by the local population that when the Army sought to relocate him to another province, the locals protested his reassignment. In a war not going well, the Army noted how rare it was for the local Vietnamese to have such loyalty to an American soldier. The Vietnamese would later award him two medals for his assistance.

David's officer evaluation says "of over fifty lieutenants currently assigned to my command, I would have to rate David number one ... he was instrumental in providing food, clothing, shelter, and medical assistance for these poor unfortunate people ... he volunteered to live with the refugees ... He was constantly exposed to danger and has been under enemy fire ... but was never discouraged or revealed any signs of fear." Will God read David's Army evaluation?

There's no greater testament to Matthew 25 than David's Army evaluation under fire, but God doesn't need to read that. God was there. He was with David, working through David, even though David often wondered where he was. I saw God with David in that Journal, even though David couldn't see him through all the darkness.

In those pages, I saw God working through the hands of his most beloved and faithful Biblical servant, a young shepherd boy named David from small town Arkansas, who risked his life under enemy fire to feed the sick and care for the poor.

What a young Army Lieutenant David could not know then, but I know now, is "that the grace would return to you" (1 Peter 1:13). Grace to answer all his prayers that the war would one day end, that Vietnam would one day prosper, that he would return home to see his wife and child (and eventually have two more), and more importantly, David's Faith was tested. But true to his name, he remained faithfully divine.

> *"This you greatly rejoice, though now for a little while, if need be, you have been grieved by various trials, that the genuineness of your faith, being much more precious than gold that perishes, though it is tested by fire, may be found to praise, honor, and glory at the revelation of Jesus Christ, whom having not seen you love. Though now you do not see Him, yet believing, you rejoice with joy inexpressible and full of glory, receiving the end of your faith—the salvation of your souls."*
> *1 Peter 1:1-16*

The Last Trial

They buried Paul Jones today. He was 51. They sent me a copy of his obituary; it was nothing I didn't already know, but out of respect for my fondness of him, they sent it knowing that I probably couldn't be at his funeral because I lived so far away.

The last time I saw Paul he was in trial. I was an in-house lawyer for Walmart and hired Paul to defend us in a high-risk personal injury trial in south Florida, a known judicial hellhole, a venue that defendants try to avoid because of runaway juries, a venue defense lawyers dread to stake their professional reputation in.

This was not the first high risk trial Paul tried for me, but it was the biggest. A young woman slipped and fell on water and had back surgery, in fact multiple back surgeries and over $300k in medical bills. She claimed she would never work again and would have more surgeries. We offered over $600k to settle but they refused and demanded $5m. I could have doubled my offer but the plaintiff refused anything less than $5m. We refused. We didn't expect to not pay anything, but we hoped the jury would be fair and not run away.

Going to trial is always tense, even for guys like Paul that had been there almost one hundred times before. Watching the eyes of a veteran trial attorney, as they make that finally walk into the courtroom, is like watching a boxer or martial artist climbing into the ring. The pressure on Paul was intense as his personal reputation was on the line and defense attorneys in particular are always worried that a big loss means the loss of a big client like Walmart.

I tried to ease Paul's tension by confirming in an email that it was my call to try this case and that I didn't expect a win, meaning a defense verdict, but Paul didn't go in there to lose. No matter the odds against him, he was there to win.

The case would last five days. Over those five days, we spent a lot of time together, eating breakfast, lunch and dinner together each day and night, and spending long nights going over the last day's evidence and the next day's witnesses, and during all that time, it's hard not to get to know someone on a deeper level. You get to hear them take phone calls from their family. Paul had a wife of 29 years and two kids that he loved. I wouldn't hear everything and tried not to, but you hear enough to see the other side of the man. You see the husband and father too.

This was not my first trial with Paul either, so over the years, I developed a great respect and admiration for this man who was as successful out of the courtroom as he was in the courtroom, a success I learned was related to his honesty, that everyone who got to know Paul, even those jurors who would sit and listen to him over the next five days, knew above all other things has wasn't a slick attorney, he was an honest man. They learned to believe in him, as did I.

For five days I sat outside the courtroom occasionally peeking through the door. I didn't want to sit in the courtroom and be a distraction to Paul. Even when the jury was out deliberating, I sat outside wanting to give Paul time to collect his thoughts and emotions before having to deliver to me the jury's verdict. Jurors are always first to leave, so I sat and watched the jurors leave before getting the news from Paul. I couldn't read their faces. The courtroom door closed behind the last juror and they shuffled onto the elevator with stoic faces. I waited for Paul.

The courtroom door opened and Paul walked to me. There was no joy or sadness in his face. He was obviously tired. "We won" he said. And by that he meant the impossible had happened. We owed nothing. Paul always believed the plaintiff was being untruthful in her testimony, and I believed him but never believed the jurors in this judicial hellhole would. But they did. They believed him too.

This was Paul's last trial. He was diagnosed with brain cancer shortly thereafter. He was buried today. He was a trial lawyer. A man I believed in, a man that all who met believed in too, even six jurors in a judicial hellhole, but more importantly, he was a husband of 29 years and a proud father of two. Paul, may God rest your soul.

Someday, but not Today

It's hard to see the big picture when tears are in your eyes.

(Our mailbox where Joe and I talk)

I saw Joe today. He was out on his daily walk. He's my 70+ year old neighbor, retired military. He walks each day and today he was walking during a break in the storm. I once saw him take a break from his walk and take my parents' trashcans from the curb back to the garage. My Dad was bedridden and dying of dementia, and my Mom rarely left the house. I caught up with Joe and thanked him for helping them. He said that's what neighbors do, and he kept walking.

Today I was out by the street getting my mail and saw him walking towards me. I waited by the mailbox to ask how his wife was doing. His second wife is dying of cancer. His first wife died of ALS the year before we moved into the neighborhood, and his almost 50-year-old son, who lives down the street, is terminally ill with cancer too.

There's a lot weighing on Joe, retirement has not been easy on him, and I could see it on his face when he stopped and shook my hand. She's not doing well he said. She's eating less than a cup of food a day and drinking only six ounces a day. I asked him if there was anything we could do.

Someday he said, but not today.

The Emergency Room Nurse

I had an early morning breakfast with my daughter. She's 24. It was breakfast for me but dinner for her. She was finishing her 12-hour shift as an emergency room nurse. She called to see if I wanted to have breakfast. Of course, I did. As our kids grow older, our time with them gets more precious as their lives seem to leave so little time for us anymore, and that's ok, that's the way it's supposed to be, so like you, I will take whatever time they can afford to give me and have breakfast with my kids anytime, anyplace, anywhere. She suggested Waffle House, because it's open during her odd hours and close to where she works.

I sat in the booth and took my first sip of coffee with her. She looked tired. She ended her shift bathing the lifeless body of a beautiful twenty-year-old woman killed in a car wreck. A guy ran a red light demolishing the car she was driving. She and her siblings had to be extricated by EMS. The ER got about five minutes notice of four in-bound trauma patients. They assembled their trauma team. For over forty-five desperate minutes, they tried to save this young woman calling out times, medicines, and then in a final moment of unusual quiet, as the team waited for any sign of life, the surgeon called it.

One of them would have to make the long walk to the waiting room and deliver the bad news to the family and someone else would have to clean the body before the family could be brought back to see their daughter one last time.

My daughter would clean the woman, a young mother. The nurse that delivered the bad news couldn't help but cry, and neither could I, for my time with that young nurse coming off her night shift was more precious than I imagined, and so is she.

The American I met

There is great freedom in letting go the burden of your own opinions

It's kinda unusual to see a middle-aged Egyptian man in the Bible belt. It's even more unusual to see a slender, middle aged, Egyptian man from Oklahoma in the Bible belt. It's really unusual to see a slender, middle aged, Egyptian man from Oklahoma walking in the Bible belt wearing a cowboy hat, wrangler jeans, and cowboy boots. And it's rare to see that same man walk into a public library in Fort Smith, Arkansas and sit down among a group of about twenty elderly white, American women for a creative writing class. Now, understand what I just said, this was a creative writing class, not a basic English class.

This class was not for those seeking to learn the basics of English grammar, but for those seeking to master the art of English story telling. For this particular class, each "student" brought a picture from home and had to write a short story about it. His story, I had to hear.

I was invited as a guest, by a friend and fellow attorney, to sit in on this creative writing class to see if there was anything I could learn. I learned more about myself than I did about writing.

I found it difficult to listen to much of what the instructor said or the stories that the other students read. My focus constantly drifted to the Egyptian cowboy sitting near me. I could see his picture sitting on the table in front of him, along with his short story. From where I sat, I couldn't tell anything about either of them, except that his story was typed. I didn't know cowboys typed. I wondered what an Egyptian cowboy would write and waited for his story. Was he really a cowboy or was he dressing up? He was quiet like a cowboy, but that may have been because he was a foreigner in a foreign land.

Finally, it was the Egyptian cowboy's turn to read. He described the picture he brought with him. It was a picture of the World Trade Center, before it was bombed. Wow, the possibilities ran wild in my mind. This Egyptian cowboy certainly had the courage of a bull rider to write a story about 9-11 in the Bible belt. This ought to be interesting. It's a good thing we were sitting in a room full of women. Maybe, he wasn't so courageous after all.

But his story wasn't about 9-11. It was titled, "The American I met." I chastised myself for being so prejudiced. When a red-blooded American male sees an Egyptian cowboy getting ready to read a story about the World Trade Center, he automatically assumes it's a story about 9-11, but he automatically assumes wrong.

His was a story about him coming to America. Funny, I never did that. Being born here, I just assumed all "Americans" were born here too, never really thinking about the first thing that most people coming to America see is New York City, its big buildings, and never having appreciated the impression that must leave.

His was a wonderful story about his first moments in America as a fifteen-year old boy, coming here from the Middle East, and the first American he met. It was beautifully written by a man that wasn't born here, who had a greater command of the English language than I did, who found the America he was looking for in the smile and face of the first American he ever met, a black man driving a bus.

Everyone was moved hearing his story, as he recounted a vision of America "we" only read in "our" history books, but this was no history book, this was the compelling story of a man sitting right next to me, today.

After he finished reading, the instructor then passed out pictures to the class and gave everyone their next assignment, which was to write a story about the picture she handed them.

The picture that she handed the Egyptian cowboy was a black and white photo of a nameless family of tough, hardy, American pioneers sitting in front of a dug-out house with a thatched roof, living somewhere "out West", in a place that had no name other than "the West", because no place had yet been named. But the names and places captured in this picture were unimportant, because the essence of the picture wasn't about those people particularly, but about the essence of a hardy people in American history that moved "west", symbolic for moving to the unknown, to forge a land we now call America. This was a picture that embodied the American spirit – the West.

We Americans treasure that picture now, like a family picture, but it was obvious to me that the Egyptian cowboy had more in common with the people in that old picture than I did. It was nice to meet an American.

Bon Appetit

Voir Dire is a French word which, no matter how highly educated, no American lawyer can pronounce it correctly by virtue of the fact that the American tongue has grown vulgar and lost its ability to taste the romance of a word well spoken. Voir Dire is a Latin phrase which means to examine a person's fitness for jury duty, and though no American lawyer can pronounce it correctly, every American lawyer proudly mispronounces it in front of a jury to sound like they learned something in law school.

On this day, there was one man who could pronounce the word correctly. He was a French Canadian called for jury duty. He said he was an artist, and his oversized unkempt suit worn with sneakers said he probably was an artist. His accent confirmed he was French. A young attractive female lawyer, newly minted out of law school, asked him if he understood English, to which he replied, in English, that he spoke five languages, which she didn't think answered her question, so she asked again if there was any reason why he wouldn't be fit to be a juror, he replied wryly "Why not?"

The young lawyer assumed he didn't understand her question, but it's always bad to assume, and in this case bad to assume that the only guy in the courtroom wearing a suit that could correctly pronounce "voir dire", who also spoke five languages, didn't understand the question. But the young lawyer assumed the French-Canadian artist did not understand her question, so she asked her question again "Is there any reason why you wouldn't be a good juror?" To which the French Canadian flippantly replied again "But why not?" Oddly, this same exchanged happened still a third time. It became clear that the Frenchman was using the famed Socratic method on his young legal adversary. She quickly moved to the next juror, an elderly man that worked at a funeral home.

The elderly man couldn't speak French but he too evaded her question by asking a question, but not of the young lawyer, but of the judge. "Your honor" he said, and his tone was cranky as his demeanor, "Can you turn the temperature up? It's colder in here than in my morgue." The other jurors chuckled.

It was lunchtime, so instead of answering the old man's question, the Judge dismissed them all for lunch with an admonishment not talk to any of the lawyers. But as they filed out of the courtroom, the little French Canadian stopped in front of the young attractive attorney, and with a bit of romanticism in his eyes, told her "Bon Appetit." She had no appetite left, not even for this trial which she had so long prepared, but not for this.

The Caveman

Yesterday morning, my cop friend called. This is not unusual as we talk almost daily. Yesterday he woke up worried about a homeless man living under a bridge. It was 18 degrees outside and he was worried that this man may not be ok, may not have survived the long cold night.

My friend climbed the steep embankment to the concrete cave where the man was known to sleep. There he was, sleeping like a caveman in an old army sleeping bag with a small dog that followed him faithfully. The man smiled at my friend with warm eyes. He said that good old army sleeping bag was toasty. He assured my friend that he was ok and needed nothing, but other than that sleeping bag and little dog, he didn't have much. My friend didn't have paper or a pen to leave his number but used his finger instead to write his cell number in the dust on the wall next to the homeless man in case he changed his mind. The man said thanks but he couldn't see well enough to read it and wouldn't need it anyway.

On this morning, I woke to read about a 42-year-old lawyer, a partner in a big Los Angeles law firm, who sat in the comfort of his car in the office parking lot, put a gun to his head, and ended it all. It would seem he had it all, but something was missing. Maybe all he needed was a cold night, a little dog, a sleeping bag and a little cave. I don't know, but one night would be worth a try.

Mothers and Lawyers

I find there is little difference between a good mother and a good lawyer. We run to either depending on where we are in life, and whichever one we run to, the best of the best are always glad to see us, always listens, exercises great patience to calm us in our hour of need, offers sage advice, corrects us when they must, and fights for us when we can't. A good lawyer is always a good mother. And a good mother is always a good lawyer.

The Killing of Billy Harvey

I once asked my Dad if he would defend someone guilty of murder. It was an innocent question from a kid worried that his Dad might be one of those seedy lawyers everyone hated, one who would get guilty people off on technicalities if you paid him enough money to do it. What began with a kid wanting assurance his Dad was good left him years later looking into his own heart, as that kid turned lawyer sat in a courtroom defending a man charged with murder.

"Dad, would you defend someone guilty of murder?"

"Well, if they are guilty, they've already been tried and convicted which means they don't need a lawyer."

It was a nice way of showing me that I was the one who was guilty - guilty of not being fair, but I was trying to learn and his kind, patient tone showed he understood.

"Well, what if he told you he did it, before he got tried, would you defend him?"

"Well, why did he do it?"

"What do you mean?"

"What was his reason for killing, that's important to know don't you think?"

He knew what I meant. I didn't mean a justified killing. Why my Dad made simple questions so difficult I never understood. But this was a lesson that words having meaning, and meaning makes all the difference to the question being asked, and justice demanded the right question be asked to get a just answer.

"Well Dad, what if he didn't have any reason, what if he just robbed a store and killed someone?"

I asked this because not long before, my Dad represented the estate of a young grocery clerk killed in a store robbery, killed by an escaped prisoner. It was a case that pained my Dad, because the "estate" was a loving young wife and baby boy left fatherless.

"So, do we kill all people who kill someone else? What if someone killed because they were driving drunk, crashed, and another drunk person in their car died. They didn't intend to kill their friend but did. Do we kill that person because they killed their friend?"

I hadn't thought about that, and he saw in my eyes that I hadn't.

"You see son, we are here to make sure a person gets a fair trial, make sure we know what happened, why it happened, and if someone did wrong, make sure that the punishment fits the crime, meaning the punishment has to be just and fair."

I thought often about our conversation, and found myself thinking about it during the trial of John Harvey, accused of murdering his brother Billy. I was defending John. It was my first murder trial. As I waited for the prosecutor to finish his unbearably long closing argument, so that I could make mine, my Dad's words "what is just and fair" reverberated through my mind. The prosecutor said John was guilty. I was getting ready to argue that he wasn't, at least not as guilty as the prosecutor said he was. I had to concede some guilt because the judge wouldn't let me argue self-defense.

How much time John would do in prison now hinged on the semantics of whether the killing was 1st degree murder, 2nd degree murder, or manslaughter. When you read the definitions of them, there wasn't a lot of articulable difference between them, thus the tone of voice and emphasis of facts used by the lawyers arguing for one or the other would make all the difference. If they believed the prosecutor, John would be guilty of 1st degree murder and spend up to the next forty years doing hard time; If it was 2nd degree murder, up to twenty years, and manslaughter, up to ten. John was going to do time; the only question was how long.

I wished my Dad was here to close it up, for he always had a way of succinctly saying things that made sense. But he wasn't here, and John sat next to me wondering what I would say. He was as sober and nervous as I was. I had written my closing down the night before and intended to follow it, but I can't say that I did, because when it was my turn to speak, I left my notes on the table and talked to the jury, because I knew my Dad would do the same. I only hoped I could do it like he could.

John had stabbed his older brother Billy to death, I confessed, but not surprisingly, the two were drunk when it happened. They were always drunk, drinking and fighting in that little house. The only thing which was surprising was it wasn't John that died. By all accounts, Billy was older and meaner, and was a mean drunk, not a happy drunk and not a sleepy drunk, a mutual friend who was there testified to that. That mutual friend said Billy was a mean drunk, that John was not, and that the friend left because Billy was starting to get mean, and he knew what that meant, there was going to be a fight and he didn't want to be there when it happened, for Billy would be angry at anyone there.

After the friend left, Billy directed his anger at the only person left, his little brother John, and gave way to the usual bullying of his younger brother. That bullying turned into a fight in the kitchen when Billy attacked John in the kitchen.

John grabbed a small pocket knife, the kind you can buy at any local store, and poked it forward to keep Billy away from him. John poked Billy one time and poked him just above the belly-button. If Billy had any belly to him, it wouldn't have done a thing, probably wouldn't even have bled, but on Billy the point of that small blade went just deep enough to pierce his aorta.

The prosecutor would have you believe that John then coldly watched Billy bleed to death on the kitchen floor before he called an ambulance, and that warrants finding him guilty of 2nd degree murder, maybe worse, but that can't be true. How do we know it's not true? Because we know the time John called the ambulance and we know the time that the ambulance arrived. The ambulance arrived within five minutes only because they lived so close to the fire station. When the paramedics found Billy, they found he still had a pulse, which means Billy was still alive, he hadn't bled out as the prosecutor says. You also heard a doctor say that he would have bled out within five minutes, all of which means, John didn't coldly watch his brother bleed out before calling an ambulance. John called the ambulance right away.

There's nothing to suggest John intended, in any way, to kill his brother. Maybe he should have run out of the house that night or called the police, but he didn't but he also didn't intend to kill him either. He didn't stab more than once, and the wound was so small it's was barely visible. It was only a quick protective jab to keep his brother away, but unfortunately, it did more than that. When he realized what he had done, he called an ambulance, surrendered to the police, and always testified truthfully about what happened that night.

The reason you are instructed on the law of manslaughter, it because this was manslaughter, nothing more, convicting him of anything more would make this crime more than it was. It was two drunk brothers, and one of those brothers was mean drunk, but not John. John wasn't mean. Those words are not mine, but the words of a mutual friend. I ask that in passing sentence, you please insure you consider all the facts that night to determine which punishment is the proper judgment for this crime.

In the end, the jury returned a verdict of manslaughter. And I was done defending a guilty man. John went to jail and the lawyer who defended a man charged with murder, me, went home thinking about what his Father told him so many years before and wondering to himself always, was it just and fair? Did I do my job?

Wanderer Above the Sea of Fog"

. . . is a famous oil painting by the Romantic German artist Casper Friedrich. It depicts a well-dressed man, cane in hand, standing on top of a lonely mountain, arguably at the pinnacle of his life, looking down into the fog below. Friedrich only depicts the back of the man, but we all know who that man is, for if he were to turn around, his face would be ours. The "Wanderer Above the Sea of Fog" is the depiction of self-reflection as we each stare into an unknown future. But for most of us, the mountains and precipices of life are not quite as majestic as Friedrich's rocky outcrop painted in oil, but are found in lowly greasy restaurants like "Waffle House."

Waffle House is a Southern "thing." It serves a cheap breakfast 24/7 every day of the year, even on God's day, Sunday, because the people that go there have often given up on God, or maybe God has given up on them, but it doesn't really matter which it is – their soul gets lost in their coffee. At Waffle House, you can sit at the old fashion counter and get splattered with hot bacon grease or grab a booth for a bit of privacy. I enjoyed the solitude of the booth. Like the famous "Wanderer Above the Sea of Fog," I perched above my morning coffee and stared into the dark abyss held within that porcelain circle of life below. I seemed to think better staring into a cup of coffee than I did aimlessly perusing through books at the bookstore.

I used to be a company lawyer with an oversized ego, inflated by an overpaying job with lush benefits, but I was laid off five months ago, and they forced me to surrender my ID badge and along with it my ego. Why was I laid off? Who knows, but it's easy to lay off a middle-aged white guy. No justification needed. History is justification enough. I was snake bit at birth - unfortunate enough to be born white when I should have been born black and born male when I should have been born female, a tail-end baby boomer when I should have been born a millennial.

What was next? Well, that's what I hoped the crystal ball of black coffee would tell me. I knew what wasn't next. I wasn't going to "hang out my own shingle" as lawyers like to say. No way I would start chasing ambulances for people demanding million-dollar representation for the price of a Sonic burger (Sonic is another Southern "thing", a restaurant where you can eat burgers within the sanctity of your car).

There's a certain Hollywood nostalgia with poor broken lawyers battling for justice. In Hollywood, the underdog lawyer always wins in the end, but that's not reality. That's just Hollywood selling more "hopium" of the great American dream that anybody can win. It is the re-telling of the old "David and Goliath" story retold ad nauseam since time immemorial, but that was about as likely for me as winning the lottery. The reality was, my life wasn't a dream nor were the lives of any number of the other poor starving lawyers I knew trying to put food on the table while walking a thin ethical line to do it. It was a balance I wouldn't pretend to make for if I did, I would surely fall into the deep chasm of poverty taking my wife and kids with me. I would not be chasing Hollywood windmills. Don Quixote I was not.

What was next if not the law? I once read about a team of explorers vying to be the first team to traverse the South Pole. They were led by a Captain named Robert Scott. In that ill-fated adventure, everything went wrong. There was a point at which failure could no longer be ignored. They were cold and starving. They didn't have enough food for everyone. One night, one brave soul left the tent and walked off into the icy dark, sat down, and froze to death. With one less mouth to feed, he thought, the others just might have a chance, and that's what he did, but he was wrong, for in the end, they all died anyway, but still, that's what heroes do, sacrifice themselves so that others may live.

  I always wondered if I had the guts to be a hero. The sound of a text message broke my concentration, and my eyes moved from the black coffee to my phone. It was my youngest daughter wanting me to come home and run with her. My jumped for joy. "Sure" I said. "I'd love to!" As I looked back into that cup of coffee, I knew one thing, I wasn't a hero who would wander into the icy cold and die. I wasn't brave enough to the hero of my life or any other. I was instead the "Wanderer Above a Sea of Fog."

"I understand"

Keep a constant watch on yourself, and put each day up for review, for what makes us evil is failing to reflect upon our own lives and learn from our past, for the plans of our future descend from the past.
Seneca, Moral Letters, 83.2

"I understand" he said. But 35 years later, I still don't, not all of it anyway.

Writing about the happy memories is easy, but what about the other memories? Those memories that aren't so happy, those moments in time which ensnare us forever, forever changing who we are, or worse, reveal who we are? What happens, when at 53 years of age, you still find yourself trapped on your high school parking lot on Friday night after school, forever trapped in time with a dear friend for the last time, who tells you "I understand"? It is the last time you will ever see him alive, the last words you will ever hear him say, because Monday night, he will put a pistol to his head and take his own life, because he has no friends left, because the last friend he had on this earth was you, and you left him by himself on the parking lot Friday night after school, and as you walk away, his final words betrayed his eyes when he said "I understand" because he didn't and neither do you, not then and not now.

A girlfriend at the time said I was never the same after that, and I'm sure that's true, because I didn't feel the same after that, not on the inside. It's hard to accept losing a good friend because I wasn't. I struggled with my "survivor's guilt" for many years after that, a pain I gladly carried inside as "just" punishment for what I had done. There's a lot of hate in that self-induced solitary confinement. I was a bit self-destructive, I think. The consolation that I was "only seventeen" didn't help much then or now, for a big part of me still is that seventeen-year-old kid standing in the parking lot with my seventeen-year-old friend who has yet to drive away for the last time.

The part I do understand now, so many years later, is the value of a lost friendship. I hope I don't lose another - not like that. I try not to. I try to always remember to get in the car and drive off together, and even if we don't have anything to say, simply enjoy cruising around town on a Friday night listening to our favorite music.

Heart of Darkness

(Me, Kilimanjaro Summit, June, 2016)

I hate to disappoint everyone, but here is the truth about my trip to Africa, straight from the Heart of Darkness.

As a kid, I read a National Geographic article about Kilimanjaro and dreamed of one day climbing to the top and seeing the Snows of Kilimanjaro, but we never end up where we think we are going. Instead of seeing the Snow, I looked into my own Heart of Darkness.

After 40 years of waiting for this trip, in my final long hours on the plane, I read Earnest Hemingway's "Snows of Kilimanjaro" and Joseph Conrad's "Heart of Darkness." Both short stories were premonitions of my future adventure and would expose the dichotomy within myself, the dichotomy of the story I would tell others of me the conquering hero and the story I would carry inside of the shame for having bought a high-priced ticket to an expose of poverty and misfortune.

In Hemingway's "The Snows of Kilimanjaro" Hemmingway writes about a man dying from gangrene in the African bush. In his final hours of life, the man laments the "would of's" and "should ofs" of his life. At fifty, I was doing the same. I was trying to cross off my bucket list an old childhood dream of climbing Kilimanjaro, so that when my body finally succumbed to the gangrene that we call old age, I would not lament never having seen "The Snows of Kilimanjaro" or what's left of them before they all melt away. If there is any good news to the trip, at least I will not go to my deathbed wishing I had visited Kilimanjaro but didn't.

Suspended in Time

I remember my father holding my hands and slowly lowering me into the deep end of the pool. It felt like the ocean to a small boy that couldn't swim. My toes clinched in excitement as they hit the cool water, then my knees shivered, and as the water crept above my chest and over my shoulders, I looked up to my father in fear. He was still there, looking down over me with a loving smile that warmed my heart. My fear dissipated and I smiled back. To this day I remain in that pool, suspended in the water, held by the memory of a father who holds my hands still, who has yet to let me go, not even from his smile.

www.ingramcontent.com/pod-product-compliance
Lightning Source LLC
Chambersburg PA
CBHW060838220526
45466CB00003B/1151